Cowboy JUMBLE

The Rootinest Tootinest Puzzles Around!

Henri Arnold,
Bob Lee,
Mike Argirion,
Jeff Knurek, &
David L. Hoyt

TRIUMPH
B O O K S

This book is available in quantity at special discounts
for your group or organization.

For further information, contact:

Triumph Books LLC
814 North Franklin Street
Chicago, Illinois 60610
Phone: (312) 337-0747
www.triumphbooks.com

Printed in U.S.A.

ISBN: 978-1-62937-355-3

Design by Sue Knopf

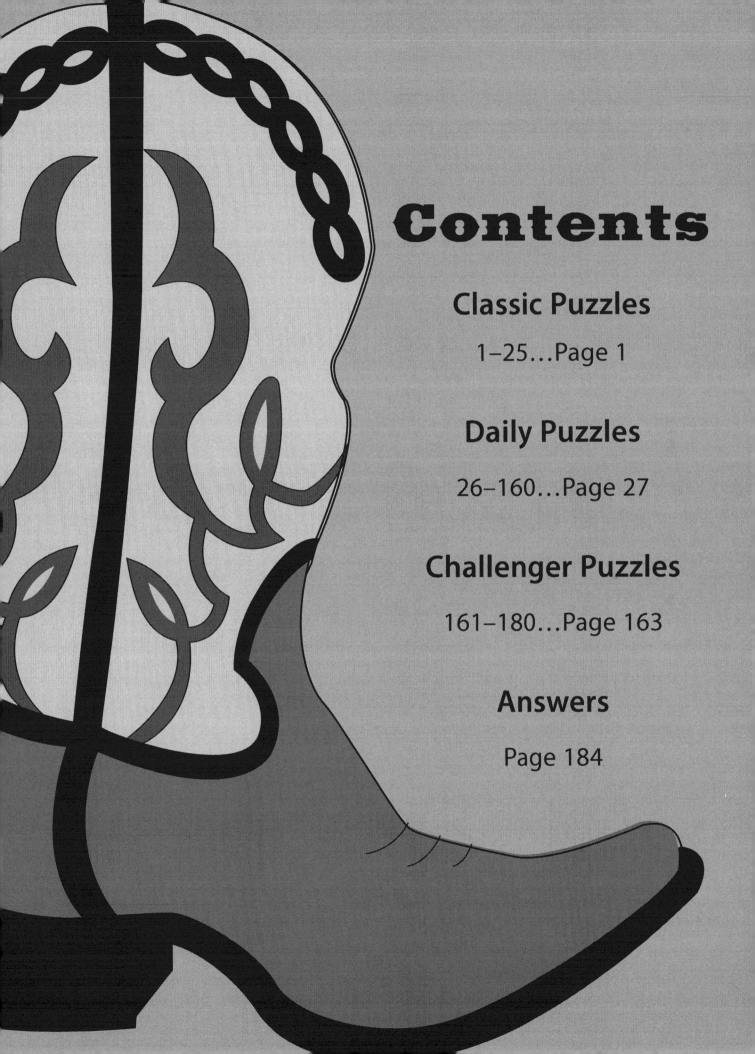

Contents

Classic Puzzles

Daily Puzzles

Challenger Puzzles

Answers

Cowboy JUMBLE®

Classic Puzzles

JUMBLE®

Unscramble these four Jumbles, one letter to each square, to form four ordinary words.

AVEEW

PUREP

KREMAT

MARFLO

Today's Guest JUMBLER is
PATRICK McDONNELL
creator of MUTTS

MUTTS © 2014 PATRICK McDonnell

THEY LOVED
THEIR ADOPTED PET---

Now arrange the circled letters to form the surprise answer, as suggested by the above cartoon.

Print answer here " ◯◯◯◯◯◯◯◯ "

JUMBLE®

Unscramble these four Jumbles, one letter
to each square, to form four ordinary words.

TREEX

FARWD

CESBIT

LOMANS

Print answer here

Today's Guest JUMBLER is
CATHY GUISEWITE
creator of CATHY

...And then the handsome prince broke the evil spell by covering her with

CHOCOLATE
KISSES

HAVING CHOCOLATE
ON HER MIND
GAVE HER ---

Now arrange the circled letters to form
the surprise answer, as suggested by the
above cartoon.

JUMBLE®

Unscramble these four Jumbles, one letter to each square, to form four ordinary words.

SLEBS

SOCRU

DEEIBS

CARYEM

THE DOGS THAT DIDN'T GET ALONG WERE —

Now arrange the circled letters to form the surprise answer, as suggested by the above cartoon.

Print answer here

JUMBLE

Unscramble these four Jumbles, one letter
to each square, to form four ordinary words.

HGILT

ALEIG

TOCLEK

NARMEN

CAN I PLAY ON THE ROOF?

CAN WE CUT WREN'S HAIR?

IS IT OKAY IF I PAINT THE COUCH?

ICE CWEAM BAFF?

WHEN THE KIDS KEPT
ASKING QUESTIONS,
THEIR MOM WAS—

Now arrange the circled letters to form
the surprise answer, as suggested by the
above cartoon.

Print answer here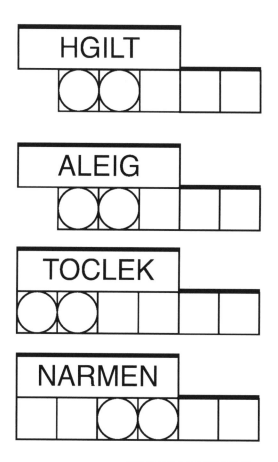

JUMBLE®

Unscramble these four Jumbles, one letter
to each square, to form four ordinary words.

INVEG

TIVDO

FAYTES

PARTUB

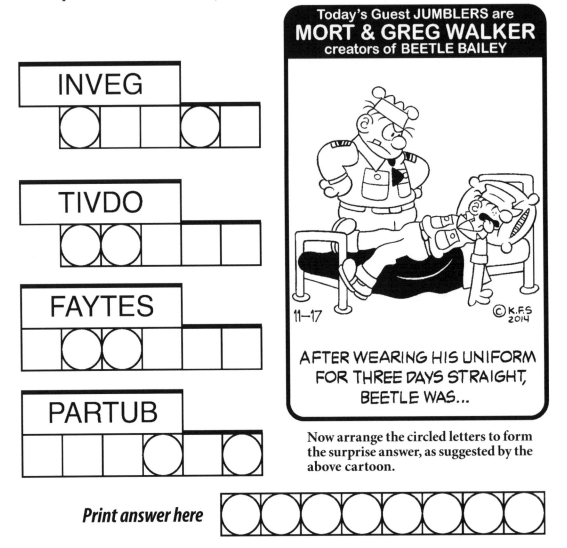

Today's Guest JUMBLERS are
MORT & GREG WALKER
creators of BEETLE BAILEY

11–17

© K.F.S
2014

AFTER WEARING HIS UNIFORM
FOR THREE DAYS STRAIGHT,
BEETLE WAS...

Now arrange the circled letters to form
the surprise answer, as suggested by the
above cartoon.

Print answer here

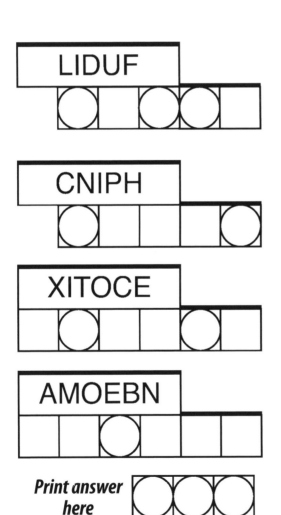

PUZZLE
6

JUMBLE®

Unscramble these four Jumbles, one letter to each square, to form four ordinary words.

LIDUF

CNIPH

XITOCE

AMOEBN

Our friend Judy is really handy too.

That's right. You should meet her.

Is that so?

THE REPAIRMAN WAS SINGLE AND HIS CUSTOMERS WANTED TO ---

Now arrange the circled letters to form the surprise answer, as suggested by the above cartoon.

Print answer here

7

JUMBLE®

Unscramble these four Jumbles, one letter
to each square, to form four ordinary words.

TAREF

FARDT

MOLPAB

GOOSET

How am I
going to fish
now?

HE WANTED TO FISH FROM
THE PIER, BUT THE MARINE
MAMMALS HAD IT ---

Now arrange the circled letters to form
the surprise answer, as suggested by the
above cartoon.

*Print answer
here*

JUMBLE®

Unscramble these four Jumbles, one letter
to each square, to form four ordinary words.

TODUB

CLAWR

NALECC

TUROPO

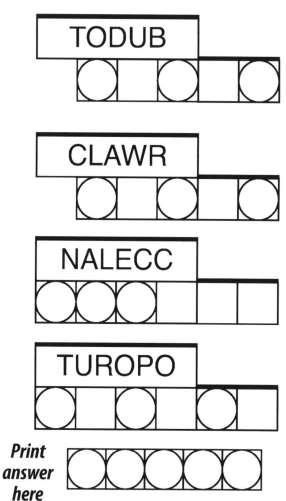

Hello, Akron!
I've come to drink
your blood!

My Life
in
TRANSYLVANIA

How many
vampires are
attending?

With you
and me,
six.

HE THOUGHT HE KNEW HOW
MANY VAMPIRES WERE THERE,
BUT HE FORGOT TO ---

Now arrange the circled letters to form
the surprise answer, as suggested by the
above cartoon.

Print
answer
here

JUMBLE®

Unscramble these four Jumbles, one letter to each square, to form four ordinary words.

YORAF

CUSKN

GLITHB

GONITU

Where's our info?

I can't believe it's not up there!

THIS SPACE AVAILABLE

LEANING TOWER OF PIZZA

PZA TWR

HE WAS TOLD HIS BILLBOARD WOULD BE UP IN TIME FOR HIS GRAND OPENING, BUT THERE WAS ---

Now arrange the circled letters to form the surprise answer, as suggested by the above cartoon.

Print answer here

JUMBLE

Unscramble these four Jumbles, one letter
to each square, to form four ordinary words.

EVAIL

HANOC

TETNEX

GONIRI

Ahhh.
This is the
afterlife.

WHEN ST. PETER TOOK A
DAY OFF FROM HIS JOB AT
THE PEARLY GATES,
HE WAS ---

Now arrange the circled letters to form
the surprise answer, as suggested by the
above cartoon.

Print answer here

JUMBLE®

Unscramble these four Jumbles, one letter
to each square, to form four ordinary words.

LEEBV

USISE

DEYMAR

FRIDAA

I'll fake an injury.
Once they open the
door, I'm outta here!

Really?
Take me!

THE EAGLE PLANNED TO
ESCAPE FROM HIS CAGE AT
THE ZOO BECAUSE HE
WANTED TO BE ----

Now arrange the circled letters to form
the surprise answer, as suggested by the
above cartoon.

*Print
answer
here*

JUMBLE®

Unscramble these four Jumbles, one letter
to each square, to form four ordinary words.

INNOO

OMYMM

GIDOIN

XCDEEE

You're not
planning on
sharing this,
are you?

WHEN THEY FOUND GOLD
IN THE CAVERN, THE OWNER
OF THE LAND SAID ----

Now arrange the circled letters to form
the surprise answer, as suggested by the
above cartoon.

*Print
answer
here*

⬡⬡⬡⬡ , ⬡⬡⬡⬡ , ⬡⬡⬡⬡

JUMBLE®

Unscramble these four Jumbles, one letter
to each square, to form four ordinary words.

LATSL

CHEEN

COINRI

LUNENF

One day
they'll put
movies on
disks to play
on computers.

No way. Using a
projector is the
only way to
watch movies.

BEFORE DVD'S, THE IDEA OF
PUTTING A WHOLE MOVIE ON
A DISC SEEMED ----

Now arrange the circled letters to form
the surprise answer, as suggested by the
above cartoon.

Print
answer
here

◯◯ - "◯◯◯◯◯" - ◯◯◯◯◯◯

JUMBLE

Unscramble these four Jumbles, one letter
to each square, to form four ordinary words.

SATHS

GIMTH

FEXRIP

FITYON

What
are you
doing?

Playing games.
There's nothing
else to do.

THE BACKUP
QUARTERBACK
WAS ---

Now arrange the circled letters to form
the surprise answer, as suggested by the
above cartoon.

*Print
answer
here*

JUMBLE®

Unscramble these four Jumbles, one letter
to each square, to form four ordinary words.

TAIDM

MUPEL

RENOYR

NAMEUH

What can
you tell
us?

I feel it was
injured in the last
storm. Once it's
over its trauma, it
will be fine.

THE TREE WASN'T GROWING
COCONUTS LIKE IT SHOULD,
AND IN ORDER TO FIND
OUT WHY, THEY HIRED A ---

Now arrange the circled letters to form
the surprise answer, as suggested by the
above cartoon.

*Print answer
here*

JUMBLE®

Unscramble these four Jumbles, one letter
to each square, to form four ordinary words.

LURTY

BEREL

SLIPHO

GUNOLE

The fruit
is just
withering
away.

I think it has too
many branches
and not enough
water.

WHEN HER PLUM TREE
DRIED UP DUE TO SUMMER
HEAT, SHE DECIDED TO ---

Now arrange the circled letters to form
the surprise answer, as suggested by the
above cartoon.

Print answer here

JUMBLE®

Unscramble these four Jumbles, one letter to each square, to form four ordinary words.

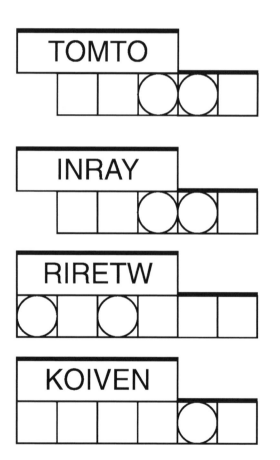

TOMTO

INRAY

RIRETW

KOIVEN

See! I made this sweater to go with my hat. I'm really getting the hang of this.

This is a sweater? Are you sure that's a hat?

SHE LET HER HUSBAND MAKE SOMETHING WITH HER YARN, BUT HE WAS A ----

Now arrange the circled letters to form the surprise answer, as suggested by the above cartoon.

Print answer here " ◯◯◯◯◯◯◯◯ "

18

JUMBLE®

Unscramble these four Jumbles, one letter to each square, to form four ordinary words.

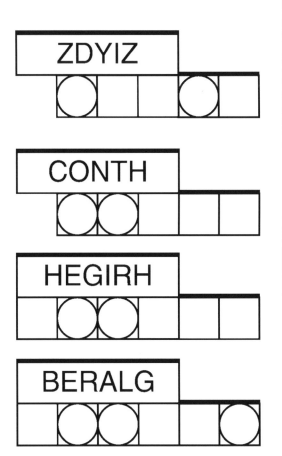

ZDYIZ

CONTH

HEGIRH

BERALG

Is everything ready to go for today's service?

I have the songs on this spreadsheet. Then, I've backed them up on my phone.

THE KEYBOARD PLAYER AT THE CHURCH WAS ---

Now arrange the circled letters to form the surprise answer, as suggested by the above cartoon.

Print answer here

JUMBLE®

Unscramble these four Jumbles, one letter
to each square, to form four ordinary words.

AZTOP

HOOTP

UNFLAT

DROPAN

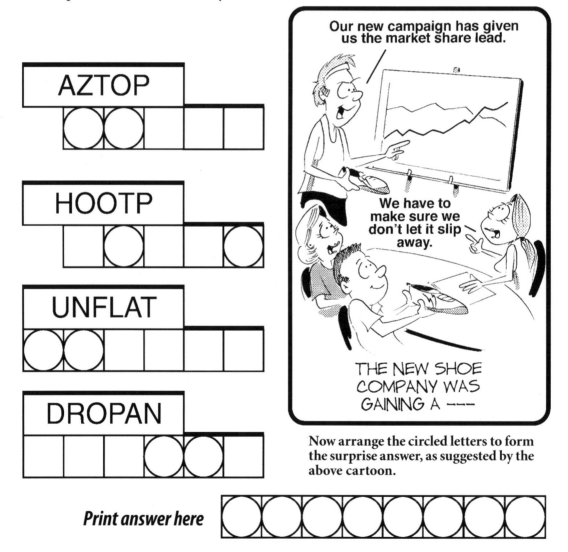

Our new campaign has given
us the market share lead.

We have to
make sure we
don't let it slip
away.

THE NEW SHOE
COMPANY WAS
GAINING A ----

Now arrange the circled letters to form
the surprise answer, as suggested by the
above cartoon.

Print answer here

20

JUMBLE®

Unscramble these four Jumbles, one letter
to each square, to form four ordinary words.

PORDO

CLUMH

LAYELG

FODBIR

These look comfortable. I wonder if these come in size 7?

Good luck getting any help from him.

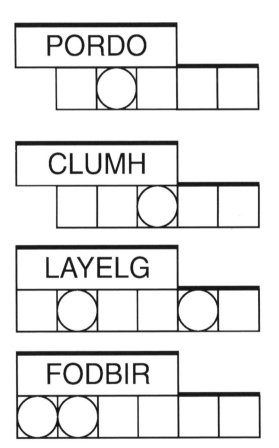

HE DIDN'T MAKE A GOOD
SHOE SALESMAN BECAUSE
HE WAS A ---

Now arrange the circled letters to form
the surprise answer, as suggested by the
above cartoon.

Print answer here

PUZZLE
21

JUMBLE

Unscramble these four Jumbles, one letter
to each square, to form four ordinary words.

HNOWS

REDNT

TAHERR

RAWNOD

It's a little loose.

I can tighten that right up for you. Need any maces, swords, or shovels?

THE KNIGHT BOUGHT
HIS ARMOR AT
THE ---

Now arrange the circled letters to form
the surprise answer, as suggested by the
above cartoon.

*Print
answer
here*
" ⬤⬤⬤⬤ - ⬤⬤⬤⬤ " ⬤⬤⬤⬤⬤

22

JUMBLE®

Unscramble these four Jumbles, one letter to each square, to form four ordinary words.

OFCRE

NARKD

TULANW

MORCEH

This is the way to start the day.

It's a little early, but at least I have my coffee.

HE MADE SCRAMBLED EGGS AT THE ---

Now arrange the circled letters to form the surprise answer, as suggested by the above cartoon.

Print answer here

JUMBLE®

Unscramble these four Jumbles, one letter
to each square, to form four ordinary words.

HYTIC

SYRIK

PUMCAS

CIDENU

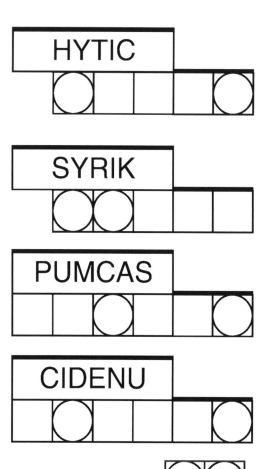

KATHY BATES AND JAMES
CAAN WERE HAPPY AS
COULD BE TO BE ---

Now arrange the circled letters to form
the surprise answer, as suggested by the
above cartoon.

Print answer here

JUMBLE®

Unscramble these four Jumbles, one letter to each square, to form four ordinary words.

MURPT

DUNEU

SORPEN

TULCAA

Let me show you how to tie your shoes so this doesn't happen again.

Isn't she a great mom?

Yes, she is.

Thank you, mommy.

THE FACT THAT SHE WAS A GOOD MOM WAS ---

Now arrange the circled letters to form the surprise answer, as suggested by the above cartoon.

Print answer here

25

JUMBLE®

Unscramble these four Jumbles, one letter
to each square, to form four ordinary words.

REEDL

BSELS

LOFTAA

OUTPOR

THE COUCH HAD
TURNED INTO A ---

Now arrange the circled letters to form
the surprise answer, as suggested by the
above cartoon.

*Print
answer
here*

Cowboy JUMBLE®

Daily
Puzzles

JUMBLE®

Unscramble these four Jumbles, one letter
to each square, to form four ordinary words.

THABC

ZALEG

DEOLDO

SACCUT

Let's try this
again. Here's
your wine and
here's your
coffee.

This is not
what I
ordered.

Are you joking
with us?

THE SERVICE AT THE
COMEDY CLUB WAS SO
BAD THAT IT WAS – – –

Now arrange the circled letters to form
the surprise answer, as suggested by the
above cartoon.

Print answer here

JUMBLE®

Unscramble these four Jumbles, one letter
to each square, to form four ordinary words.

CLEET

KALEN

FOCEFE

TOIWUT

So, how
much
to fix my
truck tire?

Trucks, cars and
motorcycles are
all the same
price. $80.

THE TIRE REPAIRMAN
CHARGED A ----

Now arrange the circled letters to form
the surprise answer, as suggested by the
above cartoon.

Print answer here

JUMBLE®

Unscramble these four Jumbles, one letter to each square, to form four ordinary words.

MBIPL

HOVES

FUNSIE

NIOIDE

Look at me. I'm the best pool cleaner ever.

Stop it! It's really annoying! Quit mocking and start helping.

WHEN HIS TWIN BROTHER STARTED MIMICKING HIM, HE WAS ---

Now arrange the circled letters to form the surprise answer, as suggested by the above cartoon.

Print answer here

JUMBLE®

Unscramble these four Jumbles, one letter
to each square, to form four ordinary words.

CHIDT

RIREV

LACAAP

TAYREE

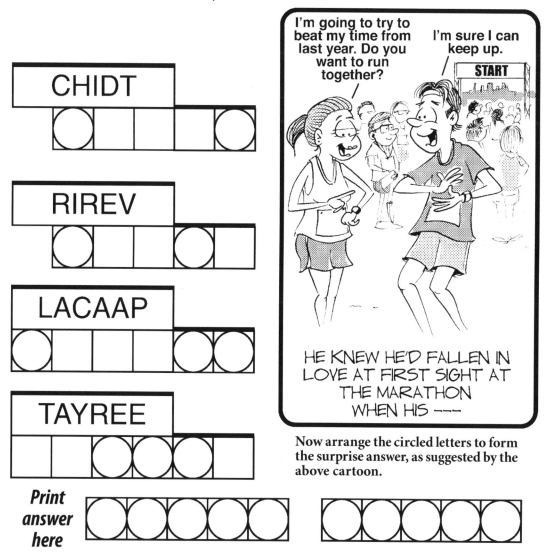

I'm going to try to
beat my time from
last year. Do you
want to run
together?

I'm sure I can
keep up.

START

HE KNEW HE'D FALLEN IN
LOVE AT FIRST SIGHT AT
THE MARATHON
WHEN HIS ---

Now arrange the circled letters to form
the surprise answer, as suggested by the
above cartoon.

Print
answer
here

JUMBLE®

Unscramble these four Jumbles, one letter
to each square, to form four ordinary words.

BEAAT

COALF

COLPUE

ROVFRE

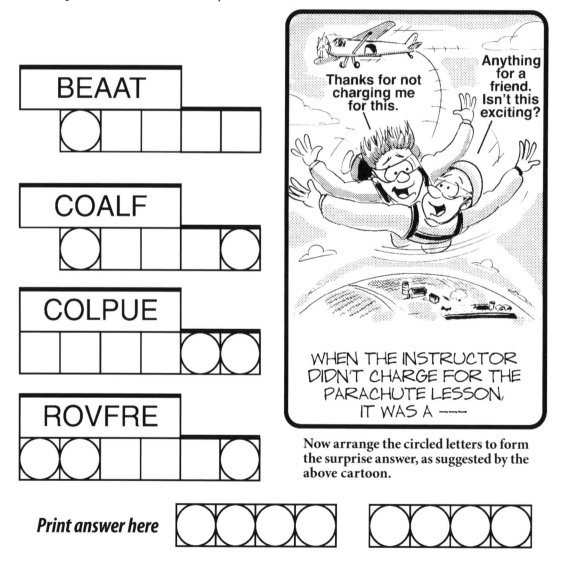

Thanks for not
charging me
for this.

Anything
for a
friend.
Isn't this
exciting?

WHEN THE INSTRUCTOR
DIDN'T CHARGE FOR THE
PARACHUTE LESSON,
IT WAS A ---

Now arrange the circled letters to form
the surprise answer, as suggested by the
above cartoon.

Print answer here

JUMBLE®

Unscramble these four Jumbles, one letter
to each square, to form four ordinary words.

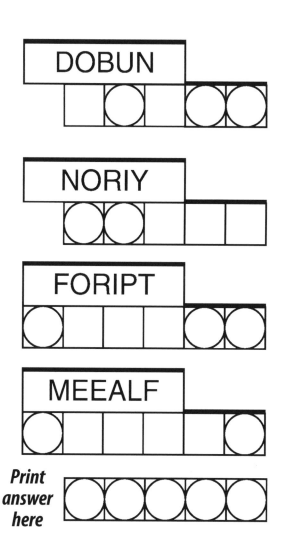

DOBUN

NORIY

FORIPT

MEEALF

So, what
do you
think?

That tree would look
beautiful in our
front yard. I wish it
was a little less
expensive, but it's
just perfect.

So, I
take it
that you
like it.

WHEN HE SPOTTED THE
PERFECT EVERGREEN TREE
AT THE NURSERY, HE ---

Now arrange the circled letters to form
the surprise answer, as suggested by the
above cartoon.

Print
answer
here

JUMBLE®

Unscramble these four Jumbles, one letter
to each square, to form four ordinary words.

GARTN

TOVEC

VINTIE

FURNIA

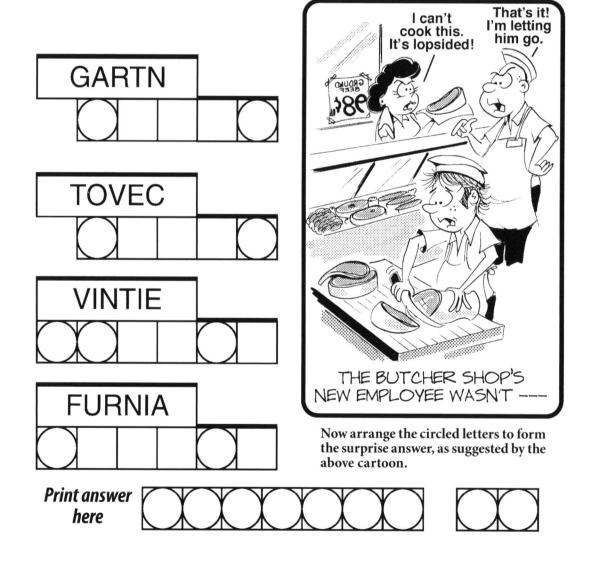

THE BUTCHER SHOP'S
NEW EMPLOYEE WASN'T ---

Now arrange the circled letters to form
the surprise answer, as suggested by the
above cartoon.

Print answer
here

JUMBLE ®

Unscramble these four Jumbles, one letter
to each square, to form four ordinary words.

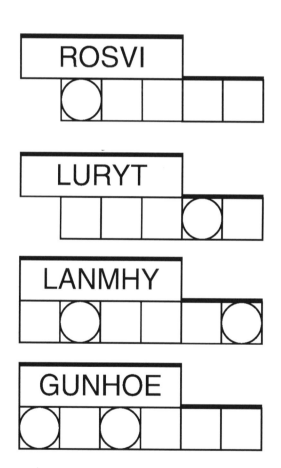

ROSVI

LURYT

LANMHY

GUNHOE

It was fun
reliving our
first date.

What a great
way to end a
perfect day.

THE COUPLE'S
VALENTINE'S DAY
WAS ---

Now arrange the circled letters to form
the surprise answer, as suggested by the
above cartoon.

Print answer here

JUMBLE®

Unscramble these four Jumbles, one letter
to each square, to form four ordinary words.

TIVDO

GOCLI

FILRYM

GEGENA

These will be the
most accurate
clocks on the
market.

Eventually, we
can expand
our line.

THE START-UP CLOCK
COMPANY WOULD BE
SUCCESSFUL ---

Now arrange the circled letters to form
the surprise answer, as suggested by the
above cartoon.

*Print
answer
here* ⬡⬡⬡ IN ⬡⬡⬡⬡ ⬡⬡⬡⬡

JUMBLE®

Unscramble these four Jumbles, one letter
to each square, to form four ordinary words.

TGIFH

DIAVO

CLOTEK

BOLGEB

I hope I get a
chance to make
one like that
tomorrow.

You
can't
miss.

KICKING THE BALL BETWEEN
THE UPRIGHTS TO WIN THE
GAME WAS HIS ---

Now arrange the circled letters to form
the surprise answer, as suggested by the
above cartoon.

*Print answer
here*

37

JUMBLE®

Unscramble these four Jumbles, one letter
to each square, to form four ordinary words.

GALEE

TINUY

BLOONG

MORRAY

I can't
wait for
the
game.

Getting the big Super
Bowl contract gave
us record profits
for the last four
quarters.

THE PENNANT COMPANY
WAS HAVING A ---

Now arrange the circled letters to form
the surprise answer, as suggested by the
above cartoon.

*Print
answer
here*

38

JUMBLE®

Unscramble these four Jumbles, one letter
to each square, to form four ordinary words.

TMAID

NEAAR

CAILIT

PENWEH

You really need to
work on your
cockney accent if
you want this role.

I'll see what
I can do.

WHEN SHE WASN'T WORKING
HER 9-TO-5 JOB, SHE
STUDIED ACTING ----

Now arrange the circled letters to form
the surprise answer, as suggested by the
above cartoon.

Print answer here ◯◯◯◯◯ - ◯◯◯◯◯

JUMBLE

Unscramble these four Jumbles, one letter
to each square, to form four ordinary words.

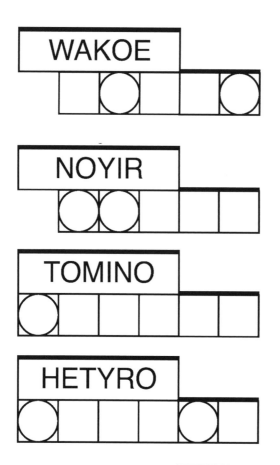

WAKOE

NOYIR

TOMINO

HETYRO

I don't mean to
scare you, but
I'm starting to
fall for you.

It will take a
lot more than
that to scare
me off.

WHEN TABITHA SPRUCE MET
STEPHEN KING IN COLLEGE,
SHE MET ---

Now arrange the circled letters to form
the surprise answer, as suggested by the
above cartoon.

Print answer here

40

JUMBLE®

Unscramble these four Jumbles, one letter
to each square, to form four ordinary words.

NEKTA

OZPAT

GINNIN

MESRUM

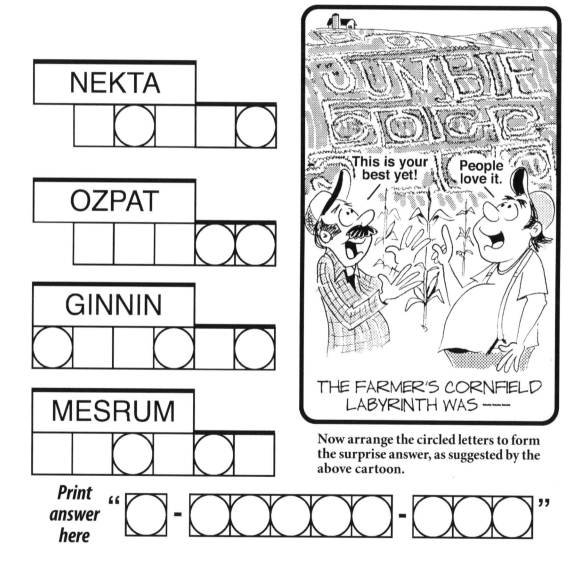

This is your best yet!

People love it.

THE FARMER'S CORNFIELD
LABYRINTH WAS ---

Now arrange the circled letters to form
the surprise answer, as suggested by the
above cartoon.

Print
answer
here

" ☐ - ☐☐☐☐☐ - ☐☐☐ "

JUMBLE®

Unscramble these four Jumbles, one letter
to each square, to form four ordinary words.

BALMU

TIGDI

TOBYAN

VIETIN

Can't they work faster? We need to get this trench filled up with water before the next attack.

I have them working as if their lives depended on it.

WHEN IT CAME TO
PROTECTING THEIR
CASTLE, THEY WERE ---

Now arrange the circled letters to form
the surprise answer, as suggested by the
above cartoon.

*Print
answer
here* " ⃝⃝⃝⃝ - ⃝⃝⃝⃝⃝⃝ "

JUMBLE®

Unscramble these four Jumbles, one letter
to each square, to form four ordinary words.

BEATA

RUPEP

RUINJE

WECRYS

What a
beautiful
view!

We'll be in
Monte Carlo
soon.

THEIR DRIVE ALONG THE
MEDITERRANEAN GAVE
THEM A CHANCE TO
ENJOY THE – – –

Now arrange the circled letters to form
the surprise answer, as suggested by the
above cartoon.

Print answer here " ◯◯◯ – ◯◯◯◯ "

43

JUMBLE

Unscramble these four Jumbles, one letter to each square, to form four ordinary words.

RIGEM

RUBBL

JOANID

NIVTEN

I said, go get me that pic-a-nic basket.

A "please" would be nice. Or, you can get your own basket.

BOO-BOO LIKED BEING YOGI'S SIDEKICK, EXCEPT WHEN YOGI WAS BEING ----

Now arrange the circled letters to form the surprise answer, as suggested by the above cartoon.

Print answer here

JUMBLE®

Unscramble these four Jumbles, one letter
to each square, to form four ordinary words.

RUCRY

NAPST

TEEQUA

ROPRAL

I think we'd
better work on
knots again.

THE NOVICE MOUNTAIN
CLIMBER NEEDED TO ---

Now arrange the circled letters to form
the surprise answer, as suggested by the
above cartoon.

Print
answer
here ⬡⬡⬡⬡⬡ THE ⬡⬡⬡⬡⬡

44

JUMBLE®

Unscramble these four Jumbles, one letter
to each square, to form four ordinary words.

LASDA

GEHED

DEECEX

FESTAY

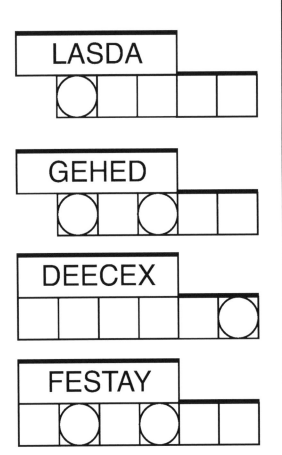

Don't worry.
I'll give
you a 5-second
head start.

Weren't you in
the Olympics?

HIS HOPE OF WINNING
THE SPRINT WAS ABOUT
TO BE ----

Now arrange the circled letters to form
the surprise answer, as suggested by the
above cartoon.

Print answer here

JUMBLE®

Unscramble these four Jumbles, one letter
to each square, to form four ordinary words.

SCEHS

LITUG

VORPEN

PETPOL

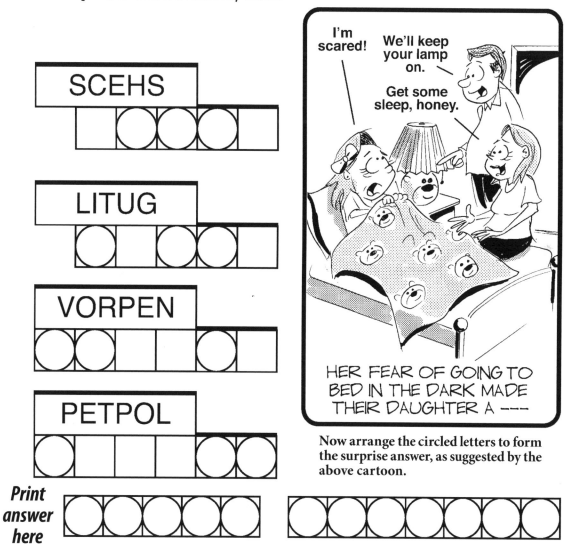

I'm
scared!

We'll keep
your lamp
on.

Get some
sleep, honey.

HER FEAR OF GOING TO
BED IN THE DARK MADE
THEIR DAUGHTER A ---

Now arrange the circled letters to form
the surprise answer, as suggested by the
above cartoon.

*Print
answer
here*

47

JUMBLE®

Unscramble these four Jumbles, one letter to each square, to form four ordinary words.

MOHOP

BAMMO

DURGET

NYLBIE

This baby was equipped with 128 kilobytes of RAM. It may have been slow, but it always worked.

CONTROL -ALT- DELETE SQUAD

Wow! That was a long time ago.

HE USED THIS TO RECALL FACTS ABOUT HIS FIRST COMPUTER.

Now arrange the circled letters to form the surprise answer, as suggested by the above cartoon.

Print answer here HIS ◯◯◯◯ ◯◯◯◯◯◯

JUMBLE®

Unscramble these four Jumbles, one letter
to each square, to form four ordinary words.

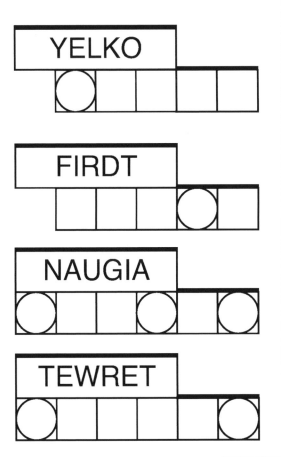

YELKO

FIRDT

NAUGIA

TEWRET

I'll go ahead and
hit while you look
for your ball.

I found it!
It's safe
after all.

YOU CAN WIN AT GOLF
WITHOUT CHEATING, IF
YOU WIN THE ----

Now arrange the circled letters to form
the surprise answer, as suggested by the
above cartoon.

Print answer here

JUMBLE®

Unscramble these four Jumbles, one letter
to each square, to form four ordinary words.

TRETU

NUKKS

NURREN

FASAIR

We have to
start charging
a fee to keep a
paramedic on
staff.

Is it
safe?

$10
Climbers
Fee

THE PARK STARTED
CHARGING FOR ROCK
CLIMBING BECAUSE IT
WASN'T ---

Now arrange the circled letters to form
the surprise answer, as suggested by the
above cartoon.

Print answer here ◯◯◯◯◯ - ◯◯◯◯

JUMBLE®

Unscramble these four Jumbles, one letter
to each square, to form four ordinary words.

PETIN

GAMIE

NEDROT

NAMLOS

Keep the water glasses
filled. Don't keep patrons
waiting for their checks.
And always say,
"Have a nice day."

Thanks for
your help.

THE EXPERIENCED
WAITRESS GAVE THE
NEW HIRE ---

Now arrange the circled letters to form
the surprise answer, as suggested by the
above cartoon.

Print answer here

JUMBLE®

Unscramble these four Jumbles, one letter
to each square, to form four ordinary words.

DUNRO

UDAIO

REHLAB

CHUPIC

I don't
think she's
going to
wait until
we land.

Don't
worry. I'm
a doctor.

WHEN SHE WENT INTO LABOR
ON THE PLANE, SHE KNEW
HER BABY WOULD BE ----

Now arrange the circled letters to form
the surprise answer, as suggested by the
above cartoon.

Print answer here ◯◯◯ - ◯◯◯◯

PUZZLE 51

JUMBLE®

Unscramble these four Jumbles, one letter to each square, to form four ordinary words.

YUPPP

SALIA

SIEWUN

GGGILE

Two down, twenty more to go.

THE ELECTRICIAN WOULD GET DONE IF HE KEPT ---

Now arrange the circled letters to form the surprise answer, as suggested by the above cartoon.

Print answer here

53

JUMBLE®

Unscramble these four Jumbles, one letter to each square, to form four ordinary words.

ZOWOY

NICGI

DAISUR

IOCCIN

THE ASTROLOGER'S
NEW BILLBOARD
WAS ---

Now arrange the circled letters to form the surprise answer, as suggested by the above cartoon.

Print answer here   A

JUMBLE®

Unscramble these four Jumbles, one letter to each square, to form four ordinary words.

KILSY

PUNIT

TENREL

LAHMNY

How are you ever going to steal it?

I'll be patient and follow him until just the right moment.

IF THE PICKPOCKET WAS GOING TO STEAL THE MAN'S POCKET WATCH, HE WOULD NEED TO ---

Now arrange the circled letters to form the surprise answer, as suggested by the above cartoon.

Print answer here

JUMBLE.

Unscramble these four Jumbles, one letter
to each square, to form four ordinary words.

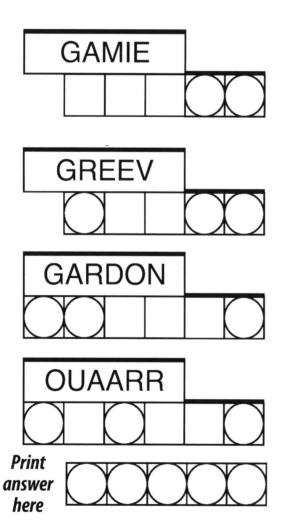

GAMIE

GREEV

GARDON

OUAARR

We need to get out of here.
That storm looks serious.

THE STORM HEADING
TOWARD THE CEMETERY
CREATED ---

Now arrange the circled letters to form
the surprise answer, as suggested by the
above cartoon.

Print
answer
here

JUMBLE®

Unscramble these four Jumbles, one letter
to each square, to form four ordinary words.

WATIA

TARIO

CALAPE

SARTHH

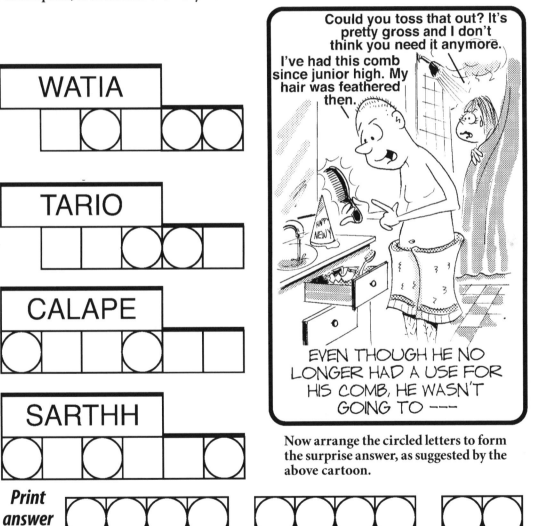

Could you toss that out? It's
pretty gross and I don't
think you need it anymore.

I've had this comb
since junior high. My
hair was feathered
then.

EVEN THOUGH HE NO
LONGER HAD A USE FOR
HIS COMB, HE WASN'T
GOING TO ---

Now arrange the circled letters to form
the surprise answer, as suggested by the
above cartoon.

*Print
answer
here*

JUMBLE®

Unscramble these four Jumbles, one letter
to each square, to form four ordinary words.

BOHYB

RULBB

FEMLUF

DENTRY

I love New Year's Eve parties. This
is great! I'm having a blast! I need
another glass of champagne!

Here
you go,
then.

She wasn't
saying much
earlier, but look
at her now

WITH EACH GLASS OF
CHAMPAGNE, THE PARTY
GUEST WAS BECOMING ----

Now arrange the circled letters to form
the surprise answer, as suggested by the
above cartoon.

**Print answer
here**

58

JUMBLE®

Unscramble these four Jumbles, one letter to each square, to form four ordinary words.

TNFOR

CEINE

OHSLUD

GIMAPE

You need to get yourself situated before you talk on the phone.

It's my wife.

WHEN HE ANSWERED HIS PHONE WHILE MOUNTAIN CLIMBING, HE SAID ---

Now arrange the circled letters to form the surprise answer, as suggested by the above cartoon.

Print answer here

JUMBLE®

Unscramble these four Jumbles, one letter
to each square, to form four ordinary words.

SUREH

VOGER

OUTAPI

GLITEP

THE WATERFOWL
IN LISBON
WERE THIS.

Now arrange the circled letters to form
the surprise answer, as suggested by the
above cartoon.

*Print
answer
here* "⟨○○○○○⟩-⟨○○○○○⟩"

JUMBLE®

Unscramble these four Jumbles, one letter
to each square, to form four ordinary words.

KMISP

NELDB

EORNUN

CLAYUN

The timer must
be off! These are
burnin' up!

WHEN THE PIG MADE
COOKIES, SHE WAS THIS.

Now arrange the circled letters to form
the surprise answer, as suggested by the
above cartoon.

Print answer here  '

JUMBLE®

Unscramble these four Jumbles, one letter
to each square, to form four ordinary words.

LUCEN

PARGH

IDARAF

KOTCEP

I can take care of all
my presents with
these.

Get ALL
4 for one
low price

THE SPECIAL ON THE
WRAPPING PAPER, BOWS,
TAPE AND SCISSORS WAS
THIS.

Now arrange the circled letters to form
the surprise answer, as suggested by the
above cartoon.

*Print
answer* A
here

JUMBLE®

Unscramble these four Jumbles, one letter to each square, to form four ordinary words.

KANEL

CROAG

REWEPT

GANNIA

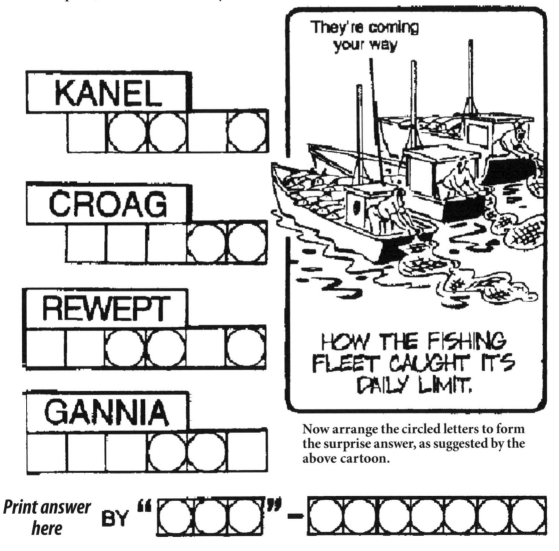

They're coming your way

HOW THE FISHING FLEET CAUGHT IT'S DAILY LIMIT.

Now arrange the circled letters to form the surprise answer, as suggested by the above cartoon.

Print answer here BY "⬡⬡⬡" – ⬡⬡⬡⬡⬡⬡⬡

JUMBLE®

Unscramble these four Jumbles, one letter
to each square, to form four ordinary words.

SYSEM

VERIP

REWESK

SILFOS

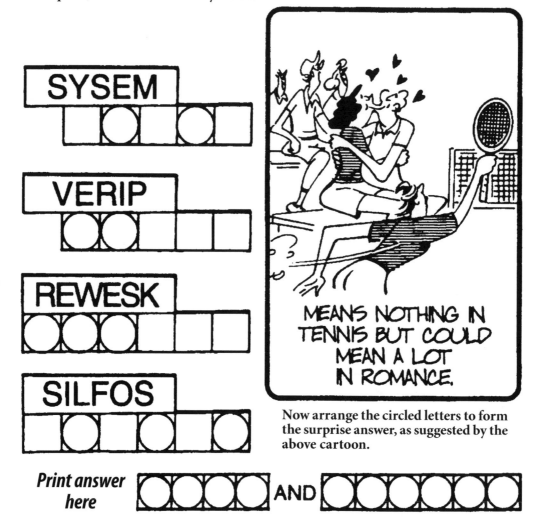

MEANS NOTHING IN
TENNIS BUT COULD
MEAN A LOT
IN ROMANCE.

Now arrange the circled letters to form
the surprise answer, as suggested by the
above cartoon.

Print answer here ◯◯◯◯◯ AND ◯◯◯◯◯◯◯

PUZZLE
63

JUMBLE®

Unscramble these four Jumbles, one letter
to each square, to form four ordinary words.

LOKEY

YALIG

YETHIG

RUTTAN

You're working
together beautifully

HOW THE CRAFT
CLASS DESCRIBED
THEIR GROUP.

Now arrange the circled letters to form
the surprise answer, as suggested by the
above cartoon.

Print answer here

65

JUMBLE®

Unscramble these four Jumbles, one letter
to each square, to form four ordinary words.

GLINY

PAMCH

YERTOP

DUNBOA

Isn't that
lovely?

WHAT THE NEWLYWEDS
CONSIDERED THE
WEDDING BELLS.

Now arrange the circled letters to form
the surprise answer, as suggested by the
above cartoon.

Print answer here ◯◯ - ◯◯◯◯◯◯◯

JUMBLE®

Unscramble these four Jumbles, one letter
to each square, to form four ordinary words.

NIHTK

LARNG

SEDGIT

AROTTE

WHAT AN UNDER-
COOKED STEAK IS IN
A SWANK RESTAURANT.

Now arrange the circled letters to form
the surprise answer, as suggested by the
above cartoon.

Print answer here A " ☐☐☐☐ " ☐☐☐☐☐

JUMBLE®

Unscramble these four Jumbles, one letter
to each square, to form four ordinary words.

WODDY

OPYPP

TIFELL

BAAMEO

WHAT SHE DID
WHEN SHE COULDN'T
MANAGE HER HAIR.

Now arrange the circled letters to form
the surprise answer, as suggested by the
above cartoon.

Print answer here ☐☐☐☐ HER ☐☐☐

JUMBLE®

Unscramble these four Jumbles, one letter
to each square, to form four ordinary words.

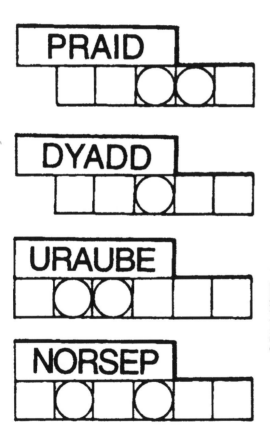

PRAID

DYADD

URAUBE

NORSEP

Drinks are on me!

If he keeps
that up, it
won't be long...

WHAT HAPPENS WHEN
YOU SPEND MONEY
LIKE WATER.

Now arrange the circled letters to form
the surprise answer, as suggested by the
above cartoon.

Print answer here IT ⬡⬡⬡⬡⬡ ⬡⬡

JUMBLE

Unscramble these four Jumbles, one letter
to each square, to form four ordinary words.

ZYCAR

MULBA

LABBED

BLOWEB

No playing until
you finish dinner

HOW MAMA'S SCOLDING
LEFT THE
YOUNG WHALE.

Now arrange the circled letters to form
the surprise answer, as suggested by the
above cartoon.

Print answer here

JUMBLE®

Unscramble these four Jumbles, one letter to each square, to form four ordinary words.

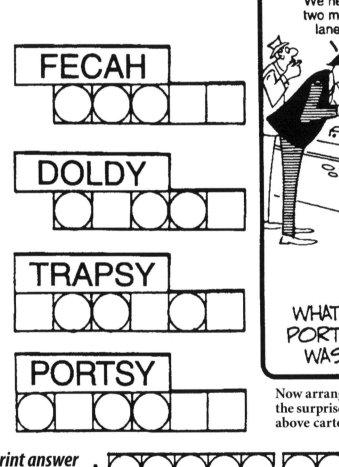

FECAH

DOLDY

TRAPSY

PORTSY

WHAT THE TRANS-PORTATION EXPERT WAS KNOWN AS.

Now arrange the circled letters to form the surprise answer, as suggested by the above cartoon.

Print answer here A

JUMBLE®

Unscramble these four Jumbles, one letter
to each square, to form four ordinary words.

YOAPS

FERIG

LINCEY

EXPLUD

THE COMPUTER
OPERATOR ATTRIBUTED
HIS BAD BACK
TO THIS.

Now arrange the circled letters to form
the surprise answer, as suggested by the
above cartoon.

Print answer here A ⬡⬡⬡⬡⬡⬡ ⬡⬡⬡⬡

JUMBLE®

Unscramble these four Jumbles, one letter
to each square, to form four ordinary words.

HUSBY

TEPIN

LORFIC

GININN

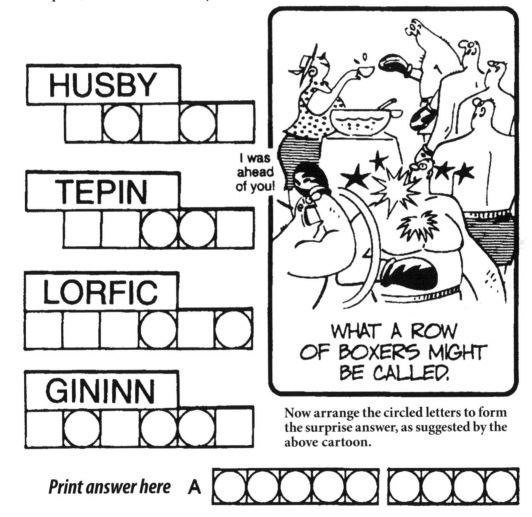

I was
ahead
of you!

WHAT A ROW
OF BOXERS MIGHT
BE CALLED.

Now arrange the circled letters to form
the surprise answer, as suggested by the
above cartoon.

Print answer here A ⬡⬡⬡⬡⬡ ⬡⬡⬡⬡

JUMBLE

Unscramble these four Jumbles, one letter
to each square, to form four ordinary words.

CUMSI

SAGYS

JELGUN

KROMES

Pass the jelly

WHAT THE MUSICIANS
OFTEN CALLED
THEIR BREAKFAST.

Now arrange the circled letters to form
the surprise answer, as suggested by the
above cartoon.

Print answer here A ⬡⬡⬡⬡ ⬡⬡⬡⬡⬡⬡⬡⬡

JUMBLE®

Unscramble these four Jumbles, one letter
to each square, to form four ordinary words.

MERIN

TEYIP

BLUESH

KIPECT

I'll do better next week

HOW THE
DETERMINED DIETER
OVERCAME HIS
WEIGHT GAIN.

Now arrange the circled letters to form
the surprise answer, as suggested by the
above cartoon.

**Print answer
here** HE ⬜⬜⬜⬜ HIS ⬜⬜⬜⬜⬜ UP

JUMBLE

Unscramble these four Jumbles, one letter to each square, to form four ordinary words.

COASH

NIFTE

TRUBLE

TENJIC

I'm asking $750 for this one

Talk about get-rich-quick!

WHY HE GOT INVOLVED IN THE BIRD BUSINESS.

Now arrange the circled letters to form the surprise answer, as suggested by the above cartoon.

Print answer here

TO ⬡⬡⬡⬡⬡⬡ HIS ⬡⬡⬡⬡

JUMBLE®

Unscramble these four Jumbles, one letter
to each square, to form four ordinary words.

TOIDI

SNAIB

SPOCER

BILBEN

This is a kind of
sea animal

HOW THE
VISITORS REACTED TO
THE SPONGE DIVER'S
LECTURE.

Now arrange the circled letters to form
the surprise answer, as suggested by the
above cartoon.

Print answer here THEY
WERE ☐☐☐☐☐☐☐☐☐

JUMBLE®

Unscramble these four Jumbles, one letter
to each square, to form four ordinary words.

KUSHY

LYDIO

CATBUD

PHELER

He certainly worked hard
for all this

WHAT IT TAKES
TO BE A
SUCCESSFUL BUTCHER.

Now arrange the circled letters to form
the surprise answer, as suggested by the
above cartoon.

Print answer here ◯◯◯◯ OF ◯◯◯◯◯

JUMBLE

Unscramble these four Jumbles, one letter to each square, to form four ordinary words.

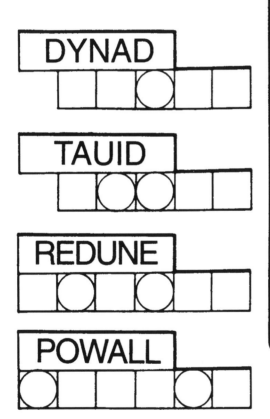

DYNAD

TAUID

REDUNE

POWALL

All caught up

WHAT THE WATCH REPAIRMAN DID IN HIS LEISURE MOMENTS.

Now arrange the circled letters to form the surprise answer, as suggested by the above cartoon.

Print answer here HE

JUMBLE®

Unscramble these four Jumbles, one letter
to each square, to form four ordinary words.

NYKAL

REBAG

DINNAL

HEYBER

Unfortunately, it was just...

OFTEN THE
EXCUSE FOR A
FENDER BENDER.

Now arrange the circled letters to form
the surprise answer, as suggested by the
above cartoon.

Print answer here A ⬡⬡⬡ ⬡⬡⬡⬡⬡

JUMBLE®

Unscramble these four Jumbles, one letter
to each square, to form four ordinary words.

YONIS

ANAFU

IROING

ERWANS

It's not quite right yet

WHAT THE
CHEF SAID HIS
APPRENTICE NEEDED
PLENTY OF.

Now arrange the circled letters to form
the surprise answer, as suggested by the
above cartoon.

Print answer here " ⬡⬡⬡⬡⬡⬡ " – ⬡⬡⬡

81

JUMBLE®

Unscramble these four Jumbles, one letter
to each square, to form four ordinary words.

TESED

SEGUS

PINGRY

NARXLY

It's a real gem

WHAT MOM
USED ON THE
KNITTED SWEATER.

Now arrange the circled letters to form
the surprise answer, as suggested by the
above cartoon.

*Print
answer
here* A ⬡⬡⬡⬡⬡⬡ OF " ⬡⬡⬡⬡⬡ "

JUMBLE®

Unscramble these four Jumbles, one letter to each square, to form four ordinary words.

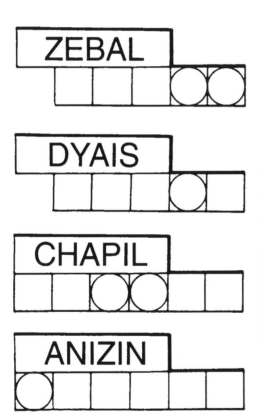

ZEBAL

DYAIS

CHAPIL

ANIZIN

Where's my order?

SOMETHING THAT COOKS DO WHEN ORDERS GET BACKED UP.

Now arrange the circled letters to form the surprise answer, as suggested by the above cartoon.

Print answer here THEY

83

JUMBLE.

Unscramble these four Jumbles, one letter
to each square, to form four ordinary words.

CALLI

THANC

CENTIE

ENGLIS

I told you to cut out that noise!

WHAT YOU SOME-
TIMES GET FROM
THE RADIO.

Now arrange the circled letters to form
the surprise answer, as suggested by the
above cartoon.

Print answer here

84

JUMBLE®

Unscramble these four Jumbles, one letter
to each square, to form four ordinary words.

PHYLS

TANCE

DITORR

NORGAD

WHY THE MEDICAL
STUDENT HAD
TROUBLE STUDYING
THE STOMACH.

Now arrange the circled letters to form
the surprise answer, as suggested by the
above cartoon.

**Print answer
here** IT
WAS ⬡⬡⬡⬡ TO ⬡⬡⬡⬡⬡⬡⬡

JUMBLE®

Unscramble these four Jumbles, one letter
to each square, to form four ordinary words.

EECIP

SHOWE

GRENED

RUSTYD

HOW THE CLEANER
FELT WHEN BUSI-
NESS GOT SLOW.

Now arrange the circled letters to form
the surprise answer, as suggested by the
above cartoon.

Print answer here ◯◯ – ◯◯◯◯◯◯◯

JUMBLE®

Unscramble these four Jumbles, one letter
to each square, to form four ordinary words.

RYTAR

LEVVA

STRAIG

RUTSLY

WHAT THE CHURCH
REMODELER DOES.

Now arrange the circled letters to form
the surprise answer, as suggested by the
above cartoon.

Print
answer   HE
here

JUMBLE®

Unscramble these four Jumbles, one letter
to each square, to form four ordinary words.

LHEVO

WOPHO

JEERTS

FITONY

Beautiful scenery

Everything's
shipshape,
sir

WHAT THEY THOUGHT
THEIR BOAT WAS.

Now arrange the circled letters to form
the surprise answer, as suggested by the
above cartoon.

Print answer here "◯◯◯" ◯◯◯◯◯◯

JUMBLE®

Unscramble these four Jumbles, one letter
to each square, to form four ordinary words.

STUJO

FAIRE

ROCENE

ENPOTT

You're better—I'll
see you in a week

HOW THE
PODIATRIST KEPT
TRACK OF HIS
PATIENTS.

Now arrange the circled letters to form
the surprise answer, as suggested by the
above cartoon.

Print answer here WITH ⃝⃝⃝⃝⃝⃝⃝⃝⃝⃝

JUMBLE®

Unscramble these four Jumbles, one letter
to each square, to form four ordinary words.

RINGO

SELOO

TRIVEN

LARREY

WHAT THE GAMBLERS
WERE DOING ON
THE CASINO BOAT.

Now arrange the circled letters to form
the surprise answer, as suggested by the
above cartoon.

**Print
answer
here**

' ON
THE

JUMBLE®

Unscramble these four Jumbles, one letter
to each square, to form four ordinary words.

PROAN

SUMEO

DUMPIO

CHUNQE

WHAT HELPED
KEEP HER DRY
IN THE RAIN.

Now arrange the circled letters to form
the surprise answer, as suggested by the
above cartoon.

Print answer here " "

91

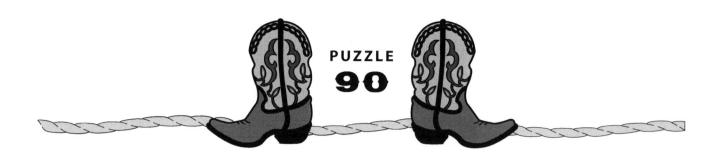

JUMBLE

Unscramble these four Jumbles, one letter
to each square, to form four ordinary words.

VIALE

IDLAY

YIRAWA

MOONAR

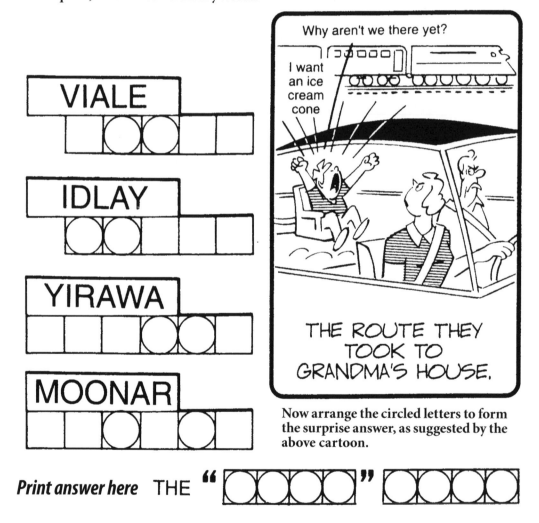

Why aren't we there yet?

I want
an ice
cream
cone

THE ROUTE THEY
TOOK TO
GRANDMA'S HOUSE.

Now arrange the circled letters to form
the surprise answer, as suggested by the
above cartoon.

Print answer here THE " ◯◯◯◯◯ " ◯◯◯◯◯

JUMBLE®

Unscramble these four Jumbles, one letter
to each square, to form four ordinary words.

ROLYG

GHEED

TORMAN

QUILID

PLAYING WITH
HER PUPPY LEFT
HER LIKE THIS.

Now arrange the circled letters to form
the surprise answer, as suggested by the
above cartoon.

Print answer here ◯◯◯ " ◯◯◯◯◯ "

JUMBLE®

Unscramble these four Jumbles, one letter to each square, to form four ordinary words.

LOPNY

SONOW

TORICE

VAHLIS

Someday we won't need to wear glasses

ANOTHER NAME FOR AN EYE DOCTOR.

Now arrange the circled letters to form the surprise answer, as suggested by the above cartoon.

Print answer here A " ⟡⟡⟡⟡⟡⟡ " – ⟡⟡⟡

JUMBLE®

Unscramble these four Jumbles, one letter
to each square, to form four ordinary words.

NAGLD

PIRRO

UNGOAT

BRUNAU

WHAT HE
CONSIDERED
HIS JOB.

Now arrange the circled letters to form
the surprise answer, as suggested by the
above cartoon.

Print answer here A ⭕⭕⭕⭕⭕

JUMBLE®

Unscramble these four Jumbles, one letter
to each square, to form four ordinary words.

HYSYL

SVORI

RYVEST

THOTEG

WHAT THE
ROMANTIC SNAKE
OFFERED THE
CUTE SERPENT.

Now arrange the circled letters to form
the surprise answer, as suggested by the
above cartoon.

Print answer here ⬜⬜⬜⬜ AND ⬜⬜⬜⬜⬜⬜

JUMBLE®

Unscramble these four Jumbles, one letter to each square, to form four ordinary words.

SOUMY

ANIFT

NATTEX

NUTJAY

THE ONLY THING THE DETECTIVE WAS INTERESTED IN.

Now arrange the circled letters to form the surprise answer, as suggested by the above cartoon.

Print answer here ⬡⬡⬡⬡ THE " ⬡⬡⬡ "

JUMBLE®

Unscramble these four Jumbles, one letter
to each square, to form four ordinary words.

TCHAB

PYKER

HABINS

DEGEWD

WHAT YOU
MIGHT CALL THE
GAMBLING SHIP'S
CARD DEALERS.

Now arrange the circled letters to form
the surprise answer, as suggested by the
above cartoon.

Print answer here

JUMBLE®

Unscramble these four Jumbles, one letter
to each square, to form four ordinary words.

LUFAW

MERGI

MAKSAD

PRUBES

WHAT THE
MILITARY MANAGED
TO ACHIEVE.

Now arrange the circled letters to form
the surprise answer, as suggested by the
above cartoon.

**Print answer
here** AN ⬡⬡⬡⬡ ⬡⬡⬡⬡⬡⬡⬡⬡

JUMBLE®

Unscramble these four Jumbles, one letter
to each square, to form four ordinary words.

METOC

ROYAF

TESVIN

DUTOXE

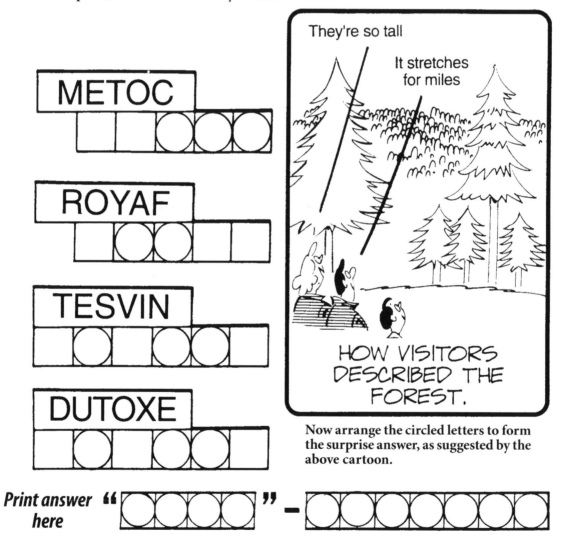

They're so tall

It stretches
for miles

HOW VISITORS
DESCRIBED THE
FOREST.

Now arrange the circled letters to form
the surprise answer, as suggested by the
above cartoon.

*Print answer
here* " ◯◯◯◯ " – ◯◯◯◯◯◯◯

JUMBLE®

Unscramble these four Jumbles, one letter
to each square, to form four ordinary words.

HASAW

ALLIV

SCETOK

JOOSUY

THE JAILER MADE
SURE THESE WERE
ALWAYS IN PLACE.

Now arrange the circled letters to form
the surprise answer, as suggested by the
above cartoon.

Print answer here

101

JUMBLE

Unscramble these four Jumbles, one letter
to each square, to form four ordinary words.

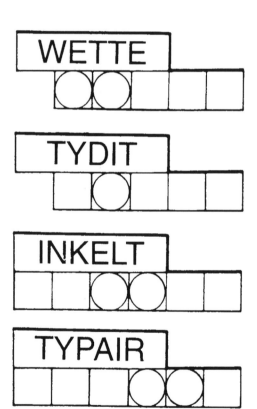

WETTE

TYDIT

INKELT

TYPAIR

WHAT THE CROCHET
CLUB CALLED
THEIR COMEDIAN.

Now arrange the circled letters to form
the surprise answer, as suggested by the
above cartoon.

Print answer here THE ◯◯◯◯◯ ◯◯◯

JUMBLE®

Unscramble these four Jumbles, one letter to each square, to form four ordinary words.

SCAMK

ROAPE

LASSIA

GOEMAH

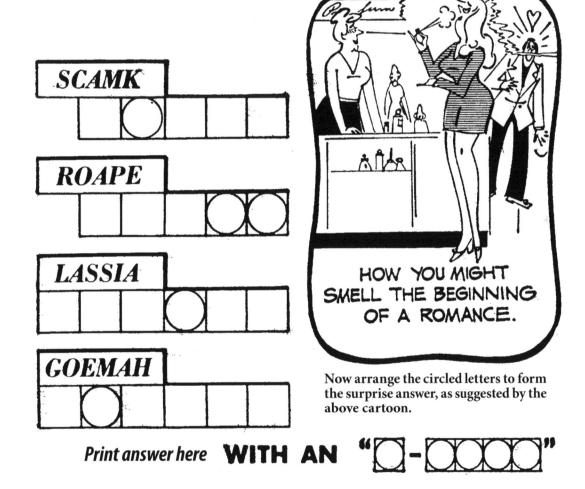

HOW YOU MIGHT SMELL THE BEGINNING OF A ROMANCE.

Now arrange the circled letters to form the surprise answer, as suggested by the above cartoon.

Print answer here WITH AN "☐-☐☐☐☐"

JUMBLE®

Unscramble these four Jumbles, one letter
to each square, to form four ordinary words.

OCCIL

KYKIN

DAUSIN

QUAPEL

Jump, miss

6-12

Now arrange the circled letters to form
the surprise answer, as suggested by the
above cartoon.

Print answer here

104

JUMBLE®

Unscramble these four Jumbles, one letter
to each square, to form four ordinary words.

CRIHB

ANGLD

TROUCY

GLAARN

I gave at the office

Will you help?

6-10

THIS IS THE LEAST
YOU CAN DO!

Now arrange the circled letters to form
the surprise answer, as suggested by the
above cartoon.

Print answer here

JUMBLE®

Unscramble these four Jumbles, one letter
to each square, to form four ordinary words.

TOOBA

CEKEH

BUHSIL

RODION

Not that dull place!

IF IT'S STILL THERE,
THERE ISN'T ANY.

Now arrange the circled letters to form
the surprise answer, as suggested by the
above cartoon.

Print answer here

106

JUMBLE®

Unscramble these four Jumbles, one letter
to each square, to form four ordinary words.

ANUDT

PAMCH

SMIBUT

TINVER

What beautiful
scenery!

BACKGROUND MATERIAL
FOR AN ARTIST.

Now arrange the circled letters to form
the surprise answer, as suggested by the
above cartoon.

Print answer here

JUMBLE®

Unscramble these four Jumbles, one letter
to each square, to form four ordinary words.

JABON

PEDYT

NAHLED

SNEFTA

Tonight again?

THEY SOMETIMES WORK
AROUND THE CLOCK
ON THE FARM.

Now arrange the circled letters to form
the surprise answer, as suggested by the
above cartoon.

Print answer here " ⬭⬭⬭⬭⬭ "

107

JUMBLE®

Unscramble these four Jumbles, one letter to each square, to form four ordinary words.

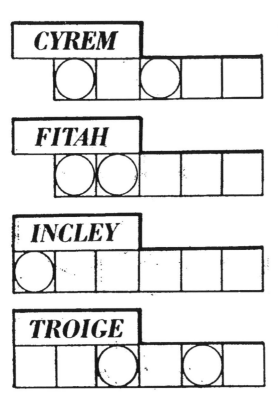

CYREM

FITAH

INCLEY

TROIGE

Hurry!

TELL THIS GUY TO GO TO BLAZES – AND YOU'LL GET A RESPONSE OUT OF HIM!

Now arrange the circled letters to form the surprise answer, as suggested by the above cartoon.

Print answer here **A**

109

JUMBLE®

Unscramble these four Jumbles, one letter
to each square, to form four ordinary words.

VENOL

PIGER

BROSAB

DAYNIT

PROVIDES THE
MAIN COURSE ON
BOARD SHIP.

Now arrange the circled letters to form
the surprise answer, as suggested by the
above cartoon.

Print answer here **THE** ⬡⬡⬡⬡⬡⬡⬡⬡⬡⬡

JUMBLE

Unscramble these four Jumbles, one letter
to each square, to form four ordinary words.

RINDE

VORLE

BOADUN

DARNBY

A PUZZLING WAY
TO MAKE HOLES.

Now arrange the circled letters to form
the surprise answer, as suggested by the
above cartoon.

Print answer here

111

JUMBLE

Unscramble these four Jumbles, one letter
to each square, to form four ordinary words.

TABEA

HARNC

INKIIB

UNPRIT

Go see him

Too much
exertion

YOU WOULDN'T WANT
TO GO TO THE
DOCTOR IF YOU
SUFFERED FROM THIS.

Now arrange the circled letters to form
the surprise answer, as suggested by the
above cartoon.

Print answer here

JUMBLE.

Unscramble these four Jumbles, one letter
to each square, to form four ordinary words.

LESOO

SILAA

TORMAN

PLOGES

Some
celebration!

FESTIVITY
WITH A GAL.

Now arrange the circled letters to form
the surprise answer, as suggested by the
above cartoon.

Print answer here ☐ ☐☐☐☐

113

JUMBLE®

Unscramble these four Jumbles, one letter
to each square, to form four ordinary words.

WONGI

KECHO

GLOANS

NICRIO

IT'S DEFINITELY
A RACKET!

Now arrange the circled letters to form
the surprise answer, as suggested by the
above cartoon.

Print answer here

114

JUMBLE®

Unscramble these four Jumbles, one letter
to each square, to form four ordinary words.

SIVOR

TEEDU

YACENG

UNRATE

WHAT THEY
DROVE BACK IN.

Now arrange the circled letters to form
the surprise answer, as suggested by the
above cartoon.

Print answer here

JUMBLE®

Unscramble these four Jumbles, one letter to each square, to form four ordinary words.

CHALT

LEEBI

KENASH

ROMMIE

MIGHT *BE* IN THE SALE AT THE FUR SHOP.

Now arrange the circled letters to form the surprise answer, as suggested by the above cartoon.

Print answer here " ⬚⬚ - ⬚ - ⬚⬚ "

JUMBLE®

Unscramble these four Jumbles, one letter
to each square, to form four ordinary words.

GOUNY

CANYF

NEPPAH

YIVELT

Regarding that shipment
of underwear—

Oops! My
wife!

5-27

MAKES MANY A SLIP!

Now arrange the circled letters to form
the surprise answer, as suggested by the
above cartoon.

Print answer here

117

JUMBLE®

Unscramble these four Jumbles, one letter
to each square, to form four ordinary words.

LOOGI

RAVOL

TALMEL

GINCHA

WHY LEAVING YOUR
OLD HOME MIGHT BE
EMOTIONALLY DISTURBING.

Now arrange the circled letters to form
the surprise answer, as suggested by the
above cartoon.

Print answer here IT'S " ⬡⬡⬡⬡⬡⬡ "

JUMBLE®

Unscramble these four Jumbles, one letter
to each square, to form four ordinary words.

NOONI

LITAP

DETHOB

HYCTOU

Gimme that!

POLITICAL DEBATE

WHAT YOU THINK
IS YOURS.

Now arrange the circled letters to form
the surprise answer, as suggested by the
above cartoon.

Print answer here

JUMBLE®

Unscramble these four Jumbles, one letter
to each square, to form four ordinary words.

YANDD

WETTE

HERBTO

TURIAL

HOW TO OFFER THEM
BETTER MEAT.

Now arrange the circled letters to form
the surprise answer, as suggested by the
above cartoon.

Print answer here "⬡⬡⬡⬡⬡⬡" ⬡⬡

JUMBLE®

Unscramble these four Jumbles, one letter
to each square, to form four ordinary words.

DRAIC

TRAFD

MIRAPI

ZYNEEM

Ready for surgery

WHAT A DOCTOR
PUTS ON BEFORE
HE STARTS WORKING.

Now arrange the circled letters to form
the surprise answer, as suggested by the
above cartoon.

Print answer here ☐☐ "☐ ☐"

121

JUMBLE®

Unscramble these four Jumbles, one letter
to each square, to form four ordinary words.

VUMEA

CITHY

RUFUTE

RYMILG

THEY DO LIKE
EACH OTHER.

Now arrange the circled letters to form
the surprise answer, as suggested by the
above cartoon.

Print answer here

122

JUMBLE®

Unscramble these four Jumbles, one letter
to each square, to form four ordinary words.

WENYL

NABOR

LENPOL

UNTAUM

Happens all
the time

COUNSELOR

MAKE NOTHING OF IT!

Now arrange the circled letters to form
the surprise answer, as suggested by the
above cartoon.

Print answer here

123

JUMBLE®

Unscramble these four Jumbles, one letter
to each square, to form four ordinary words.

RODOP

LUTEX

WEABER

UMLOVE

THIS IS OWING
TO BEING LATE.

Now arrange the circled letters to form
the surprise answer, as suggested by the
above cartoon.

Print answer here

JUMBLE®

Unscramble these four Jumbles, one letter
to each square, to form four ordinary words.

SUMIC

PETIR

NAWDDE

ENIAMA

WHAT YOU'D EXPECT
FROM A LITTLE DEVIL

Now arrange the circled letters to form
the surprise answer, as suggested by the
above cartoon.

Print answer here "◯◯◯ – ◯◯◯◯◯◯"

JUMBLE®

Unscramble these four Jumbles, one letter
to each square, to form four ordinary words.

USVEA

DYNAH

WERDOP

QUILID

WHAT A TOP HAT
MIGHT MAKE.

Now arrange the circled letters to form
the surprise answer, as suggested by the
above cartoon.

Print answer here **YOUR** ⬡⬡⬡⬡ ⬡⬡⬡⬡

JUMBLE®

Unscramble these four Jumbles, one letter
to each square, to form four ordinary words.

EVVER

OTTOH

CEIVED

RABENN

Jury is back

TRY AND GIVE THIS
TO A PRISONER.

Now arrange the circled letters to form
the surprise answer, as suggested by the
above cartoon.

Print answer here ◯◯◯ ◯◯◯◯◯◯◯

JUMBLE®

Unscramble these four Jumbles, one letter
to each square, to form four ordinary words.

COPHE

PRAAT

BATEEK

ORFALL

Fire the man responsible for this!

NEW DISCLOSURES

MIGHT MEAN SOME
DRIP LET THE
SECRETS OUT.

Now arrange the circled letters to form
the surprise answer, as suggested by the
above cartoon.

Print answer here ☐ " ☐☐☐☐ "

JUMBLE®

Unscramble these four Jumbles, one letter
to each square, to form four ordinary words.

TEAHB

YEEPA

DOULCY

EXCOIB

RAN DOWN
THE BEACH.

Now arrange the circled letters to form
the surprise answer, as suggested by the
above cartoon.

Print answer here

JUMBLE®

Unscramble these four Jumbles, one letter
to each square, to form four ordinary words.

NITLE

VENAH

HARXOT

BALMOG

Mismatched

AS LONG AS YOU ARE —
IT'S YOURS.

Now arrange the circled letters to form
the surprise answer, as suggested by the
above cartoon.

Print answer here

JUMBLE®

Unscramble these four Jumbles, one letter
to each square, to form four ordinary words.

STULY

ENFEC

ORSOUP

LISGRY

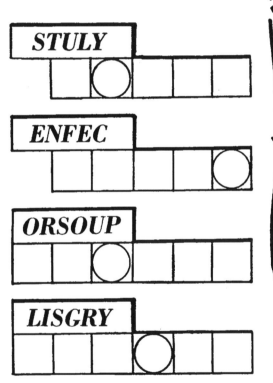

Sick friend

I'll be here

BAR

Just as I thought!

FROM A RUSE,
YOU CAN MAKE
CERTAIN OF THIS.

Now arrange the circled letters to form
the surprise answer, as suggested by the
above cartoon.

Print answer here

JUMBLE®

Unscramble these four Jumbles, one letter
to each square, to form four ordinary words.

MUPIO

NOJEY

TRALEY

DRIZAL

Huh?

ONCE AROUSED
YOU MAY LOSE IT!

Now arrange the circled letters to form
the surprise answer, as suggested by the
above cartoon.

Print answer here

JUMBLE®

Unscramble these four Jumbles, one letter
to each square, to form four ordinary words.

BROEP

DRATY

LADLAB

BONGIB

WHAT HE WAS WAS
APPARENT.

Now arrange the circled letters to form
the surprise answer, as suggested by the
above cartoon.

Print answer here

JUMBLE®

Unscramble these four Jumbles, one letter
to each square, to form four ordinary words.

GUBEN

ORVAS

SHRAIG.

TORFIP

I've got it!

TODAY'S ANSWER WILL
DAWN ON YOU
TOMORROW.

Now arrange the circled letters to form
the surprise answer, as suggested by the
above cartoon.

Print answer here

134

JUMBLE.

Unscramble these four Jumbles, one letter
to each square, to form four ordinary words.

PRUTE

AGGUE

SPRAYT

COMINE

What's it say?

They're so dirty

ACHOO!

THEY MIGHT BE
CARRIED BY CARDS.

Now arrange the circled letters to form
the surprise answer, as suggested by the
above cartoon.

Print answer here

JUMBLE®

Unscramble these four Jumbles, one letter
to each square, to form four ordinary words.

UMBOX

DEKIN

UCCSAU

FLARTE

You can see it in the dark

THIS MIGHT BE
COMPOSED OF
MUD AND AIR.

Now arrange the circled letters to form
the surprise answer, as suggested by the
above cartoon.

Print answer here

JUMBLE®

Unscramble these four Jumbles, one letter
to each square, to form four ordinary words.

KEWOA

INORM

TINCLE

TOBENN

4-27

YOU JUST CAN'T
SHUT YOUR EYES
TO THIS!

Now arrange the circled letters to form
the surprise answer, as suggested by the
above cartoon.

Print answer here

137

JUMBLE®

Unscramble these four Jumbles, one letter
to each square, to form four ordinary words.

YASID

RECEL

OURSEA

DRUTSY

Here are your notes

THEY INSURE THE
CORRECT DELIVERY
OF SPEECHES.

Now arrange the circled letters to form
the surprise answer, as suggested by the
above cartoon.

Print answer here

JUMBLE®

Unscramble these four Jumbles, one letter
to each square, to form four ordinary words.

LIVIG

KNAWE

HERTHS

WEARLY

THIS VIEW MAY HELP
YOU GET A JOB.

Now arrange the circled letters to form
the surprise answer, as suggested by the
above cartoon.

Print answer here **AN**

JUMBLE®

Unscramble these four Jumbles, one letter to each square, to form four ordinary words.

TAIRE

LUVEA

REEWKS

HABLEC

Flour next

JUST MARRIED

MIGHT BE STRAINING TO DO A JOB.

Now arrange the circled letters to form the surprise answer, as suggested by the above cartoon.

Print answer here

JUMBLE®

Unscramble these four Jumbles, one letter
to each square, to form four ordinary words.

YIRDT

GANGI

CADILP

INLOIV

His total alibi
blah blah . . .

THIS IS USED IN
SUMMING UP.

Now arrange the circled letters to form
the surprise answer, as suggested by the
above cartoon.

Print answer here

JUMBLE®

Unscramble these four Jumbles, one letter
to each square, to form four ordinary words.

IPPUL

LOVEH

SCUSID

RAZTUQ

He charges
too much

THIS WOULD DESCRIBE A
HIGH-SPIRITED CHISELER.

Now arrange the circled letters to form
the surprise answer, as suggested by the
above cartoon.

Print answer here " ◯◯◯◯◯◯◯ "

JUMBLE®

Unscramble these four Jumbles, one letter
to each square, to form four ordinary words.

USOED

GINOR

FLOAFY

RAYPER

WHAT MIGHT BE HIDDEN
IN A GARDEN?

Now arrange the circled letters to form
the surprise answer, as suggested by the
above cartoon.

Print answer here

143

JUMBLE

Unscramble these four Jumbles, one letter
to each square, to form four ordinary words.

MEFAD

VONEY

CLOTUC

LUPPIT

Who's next,
Lucrezia?

Him!

SOMETIMES CARRIES
POISON AND SOUNDS
AWFUL.

Now arrange the circled letters to form
the surprise answer, as suggested by the
above cartoon.

Print answer here " ◯◯◯◯ "

JUMBLE®

Unscramble these four Jumbles, one letter
to each square, to form four ordinary words.

TIELE

SLARN

POATIE

ROTRAM

Is this the place for the opening?

GALLERY

THEATER PERFORMANCES
NOT OPEN TO THE PUBLIC.

Now arrange the circled letters to form
the surprise answer, as suggested by the
above cartoon.

Print answer here

JUMBLE®

Unscramble these four Jumbles, one letter
to each square, to form four ordinary words.

NYKAL

FARIE

RATVAC

LICKEF

PAYMASTER

YOU HAVE TO BE IT
WITH THE FIRST LETTER
BEFORE YOU CAN BE IT
WITHOUT THE FIRST.

Now arrange the circled letters to form
the surprise answer, as suggested by the
above cartoon.

Print answer here ☐ – ☐☐☐☐☐☐☐

JUMBLE

Unscramble these four Jumbles, one letter
to each square, to form four ordinary words.

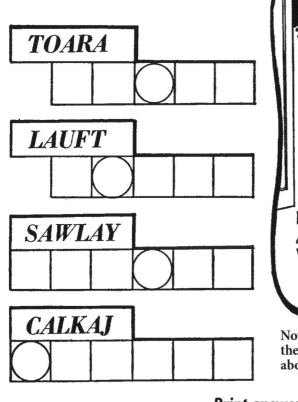

TOARA

LAUFT

SAWLAY

CALKAJ

HOW NOT TO LEAVE
A DOOR IF YOU DON'T
WANT THEM TO STEAL
A VASE.

Now arrange the circled letters to form
the surprise answer, as suggested by the
above cartoon.

Print answer here " ☐ - ☐☐☐ "

JUMBLE®

Unscramble these four Jumbles, one letter
to each square, to form four ordinary words.

TADAP

NALTS

LUPCOE

YARROS

BEAUTY   PARLO

HOW TO GET
GOOD LOOKS.

Now arrange the circled letters to form
the surprise answer, as suggested by the
above cartoon.

Print answer here

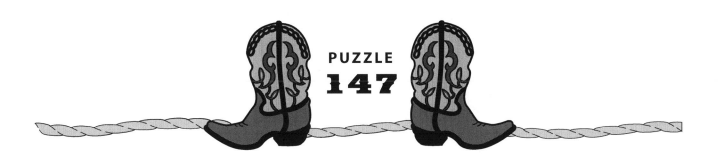
JUMBLE®

Unscramble these four Jumbles, one letter
to each square, to form four ordinary words.

KIRPE

TUSEG

SIEMUS

NUHRGY

CAR
RENTAL
AGENCY

THEY CONTRACT TO
GIVE YOU A
COMFORTABLE RIDE.

Now arrange the circled letters to form
the surprise answer, as suggested by the
above cartoon.

Print answer here

JUMBLE®

Unscramble these four Jumbles, one letter
to each square, to form four ordinary words.

CILRY

VORAF

TANUBE

DEEMLY

I love 'em all!

HOW THE FAT
MAN SPOKE.

Now arrange the circled letters to form
the surprise answer, as suggested by the
above cartoon.

Print answer here

JUMBLE®

Unscramble these four Jumbles, one letter
to each square, to form four ordinary words.

DRUIL

PAWMS

VALERM

HIPLAC

INQUIRIES

COMPLETELY TIED UP IN
POSTAL REGULATIONS!

Now arrange the circled letters to form
the surprise answer, as suggested by the
above cartoon.

Print answer here

JUMBLE®

Unscramble these four Jumbles, one letter
to each square, to form four ordinary words.

YOIRN

USTEA

SEPPIN

FAINAR

GOES OFF TO
REPORT TROUBLE.

Now arrange the circled letters to form
the surprise answer, as suggested by the
above cartoon.

Print answer here

152

JUMBLE®

Unscramble these four Jumbles, one letter to each square, to form four ordinary words.

FECOR

ROBAR

WARMOR

GEPLED

MIGHT BE MAD
ABOUT THE ENGINE.

Now arrange the circled letters to form the surprise answer, as suggested by the above cartoon.

Print answer here "◯◯◯◯"

JUMBLE®

Unscramble these four Jumbles, one letter
to each square, to form four ordinary words.

LAUNN

STUCO

GARSIT

DAIMWY

Oh, sir!!!

IT'S MORE USUAL
TO HAVE ONLY
HALF OF THIS.

Now arrange the circled letters to form
the surprise answer, as suggested by the
above cartoon.

Print answer here

JUMBLE®

Unscramble these four Jumbles, one letter
to each square, to form four ordinary words.

UGAVE

LIRLT

TAYFUL

BOICED

It's about time!

THIS WOULD INDICATE
THAT SOMEONE HAS
JUST STOPPED SMOKING.

Now arrange the circled letters to form
the surprise answer, as suggested by the
above cartoon.

Print answer here **A**

JUMBLE®

Unscramble these four Jumbles, one letter
to each square, to form four ordinary words.

FYFAT

DOREL

HUPNAC

ZEBRAL

MUSIC

THIS IS THE RESULT OF
A MUSICAL STRIKE.

Now arrange the circled letters to form
the surprise answer, as suggested by the
above cartoon.

Print answer here

156

JUMBLE®

Unscramble these four Jumbles, one letter
to each square, to form four ordinary words.

HIEWL

MOGAD

NICCIP

CHOROB

WHY SHE MARRIED
THE ARTIST.

Now arrange the circled letters to form
the surprise answer, as suggested by the
above cartoon.

Print answer here SHE WAS ⬡⬡⬡⬡⬡ TO ⬡⬡⬡

JUMBLE®

Unscramble these four Jumbles, one letter to each square, to form four ordinary words.

DOEPT

NEALK

BROIMD

EPALUG

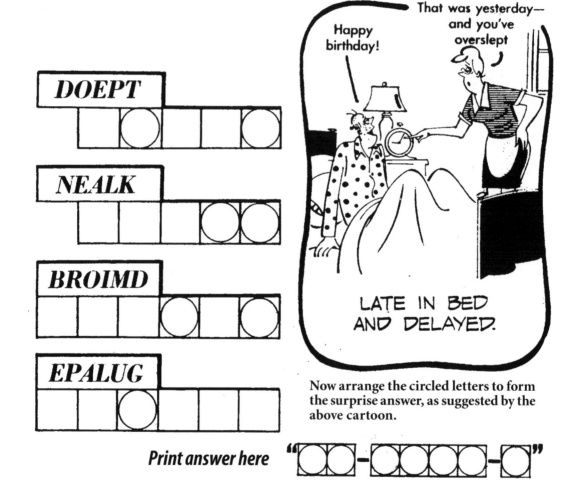

Happy birthday!

That was yesterday—and you've overslept

LATE IN BED AND DELAYED.

Now arrange the circled letters to form the surprise answer, as suggested by the above cartoon.

Print answer here "□□-□□□□□-□"

JUMBLE®

Unscramble these four Jumbles, one letter
to each square, to form four ordinary words.

HARCI

APITO

SUFOAM

GAMNEA

MATERNITY

Thanks
Thanks

TWICE A MOTHER.

Now arrange the circled letters to form
the surprise answer, as suggested by the
above cartoon.

Print answer here

JUMBLE®

Unscramble these four Jumbles, one letter to each square, to form four ordinary words.

MARAD

NILOG

DROMEN

REELCY

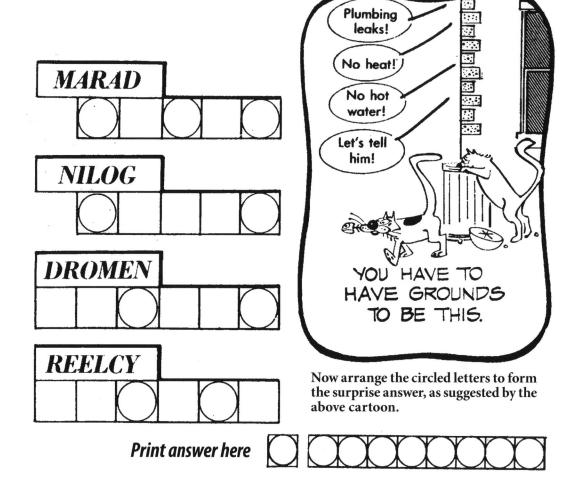

Plumbing leaks!

No heat!

No hot water!

Let's tell him!

YOU HAVE TO HAVE GROUNDS TO BE THIS.

Now arrange the circled letters to form the surprise answer, as suggested by the above cartoon.

Print answer here

JUMBLE®

Unscramble these four Jumbles, one letter to each square, to form four ordinary words.

DUGEN

YANON

HIRCUN

DILERB

Not tonight—maybe tomorrow

WHAT THE FRUSTRATED RACEHORSE WAS ALWAYS GETTING.

Now arrange the circled letters to form the surprise answer, as suggested by the above cartoon.

Print answer here **THE**

161

JUMBLE®

Unscramble these four Jumbles, one letter to each square, to form four ordinary words.

SWOHE

TYPAR

CONIVE

INNACE

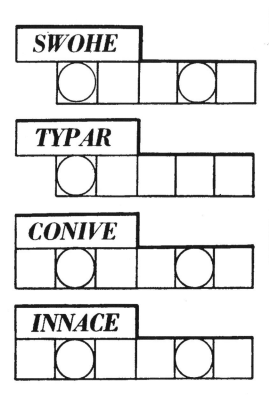

THIS MIGHT BE RESPONSIBLE FOR A CERTAIN COOLNESS AT THE TOP.

Now arrange the circled letters to form the surprise answer, as suggested by the above cartoon.

Print answer here

Cowboy JUMBLE®

Challenger
Puzzles

JUMBLE®

Unscramble these six Jumbles, one letter to each square, to form six ordinary words.

SUWENI

GRULFA

WHRONT

INIDOE

PLUCTS

OLATAF

The enemy is going to be here by nightfall.

If this doesn't work, we're in trouble.

This better work.

BUILDING A MOAT AROUND THE CASTLE WAS A ----

Now arrange the circled letters to form the surprise answer, as suggested by the above cartoon.

Print answer here

JUMBLE

Unscramble these six Jumbles, one letter
to each square, to form six ordinary words.

VITREH

KENOYD

MIFYAN

TEFSAY

STARHH

XEPLUD

YES!

If he makes
this, he has
a good
chance of
winning.

SINKING THE 50-FOOTER
FOR EAGLE ---

Now arrange the circled letters to form
the surprise answer, as suggested by the
above cartoon.

Print answer here

" ◯◯◯◯ " ◯◯◯ ◯◯ ◯◯◯ ◯◯◯◯

JUMBLE

Unscramble these six Jumbles, one letter to each square, to form six ordinary words.

MUMNIE

RAHMEM

MIDOSW

BEMNIL

TORFAM

TAVNAC

I can't believe I have a son. This is so wonderful. What shall we name him?

Let's call him Bambi. He's just so cute. I can't keep my hooves off of him.

Don't you think that's kind of a girly name?

AFTER THE DEER HAD A BABY, THEY ———

Now arrange the circled letters to form the surprise answer, as suggested by the above cartoon.

Print answer here

JUMBLE®

Unscramble these six Jumbles, one letter to each square, to form six ordinary words.

DHAIRS

VERITH

ELCAAP

SCENTH

CESLOT

SWUNIE

It's a beautiful day. You deserve some sun and relaxation.

I called the station. I told them I was sick. I hope I don't get in trouble.

THE METEOROLOGIST CALLED IN TO WORK SICK SO THAT SHE COULD GET ----

Now arrange the circled letters to form the surprise answer, as suggested by the above cartoon.

Print answer here

JUMBLE®

Unscramble these six Jumbles, one letter
to each square, to form six ordinary words.

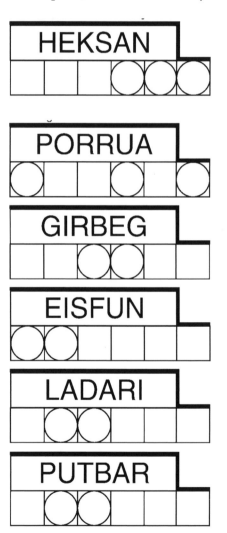

HEKSAN

PORRUA

GIRBEG

EISFUN

LADARI

PUTBAR

You can see it repeatedly smashes the rock.

I've never seen anything like this!

This will change excavating forever.

WHEN THE JACKHAMMER
WAS INVENTED,
IT WAS ---

Now arrange the circled letters to form
the surprise answer, as suggested by the
above cartoon.

Print answer here

JUMBLE®

Unscramble these six Jumbles, one letter to each square, to form six ordinary words.

SANVIH

HERRAD

GEGNEA

GRECLY

ROMLAT

SOMUTT

So, do you love them?

They are amazing!

SHOE SALE

WHEN IT CAME TO THE NEW PAIR OF SHOES, SHE WAS ---

Now arrange the circled letters to form the surprise answer, as suggested by the above cartoon.

Print answer here

◯◯◯◯ ◯◯◯◯ ◯◯◯◯◯

JUMBLE®

Unscramble these six Jumbles, one letter to each square, to form six ordinary words.

RESYUV

SENRUU

HETROY

STWACH

RULUNY

VOSYAR

AFTER SUCH A DREARY WINTER AND WET SPRING, THE DAD WAS HAPPY TO SEE SOME ---

Now arrange the circled letters to form the surprise answer, as suggested by the above cartoon.

Print answer here

" ☐☐☐☐☐ " ☐☐☐☐☐☐☐☐

170

JUMBLE®

Unscramble these six Jumbles, one letter
to each square, to form six ordinary words.

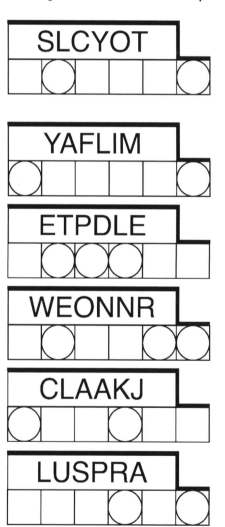

SLCYOT

YAFLIM

ETPDLE

WEONNR

CLAAKJ

LUSPRA

Ironically, this is the best way for us to travel.

It's like this whether we leave from LaGuardia or JFK.

12

WHEN THE GIANTS
LEAVE THE BIG APPLE
FOR AN AWAY GAME,
THEY ---

Now arrange the circled letters to form
the surprise answer, as suggested by the
above cartoon.

Print answer here

JUMBLE®

Unscramble these six Jumbles, one letter to each square, to form six ordinary words.

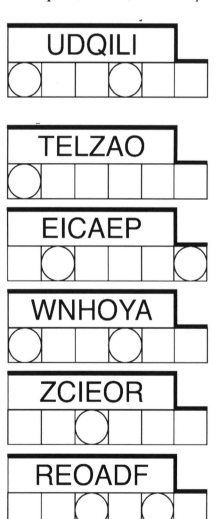

UDQILI

TELZAO

EICAEP

WNHOYA

ZCIEOR

REOADF

WHEN THEY CARVED THE JUMBLE INTO GRANITE, THEY MADE A ----

Now arrange the circled letters to form the surprise answer, as suggested by the above cartoon.

Print answer here

JUMBLE®

Unscramble these six Jumbles, one letter to each square, to form six ordinary words.

QAICUT

PRAGAM

RKTYIC

PRTINU

CPIUPK

RWERIT

I'm sure glad we brought the camera!

Sydney, do you remember riding the waves?

Look at the sandcastle I built.

TAKING PHOTOGRAPHS OF YOUR VACATION MAKES IT EASIER TO DO THIS LATER.

Now arrange the circled letters to form the surprise answer, as suggested by the above cartoon.

Print answer here

173

JUMBLE®

Unscramble these six Jumbles, one letter to each square, to form six ordinary words.

VIRTED

JURNIY

TOXREV

BUCTAD

PARTTE

OWWINN

The flight is cancelled

WHAT THE PASSENGERS EXPERIENCED WHEN THE SNOWSTORM HIT.

Now arrange the circled letters to form the surprise answer, as suggested by the above cartoon.

Print answer here

A " ◯◯◯◯◯◯ - ◯◯◯◯◯ "

JUMBLE®

Unscramble these six Jumbles, one letter to each square, to form six ordinary words.

PEKAUM

PECDIT

RAYVOS

HUBERC

CHERIP

NARROC

Do you have an account with us?

WHAT A BANK TELLER WILL DO BEFORE SHE'LL CASH YOUR CHECK.

09-26-10

Now arrange the circled letters to form the surprise answer, as suggested by the above cartoon.

Print answer here

JUMBLE®

Unscramble these six Jumbles, one letter to each square, to form six ordinary words.

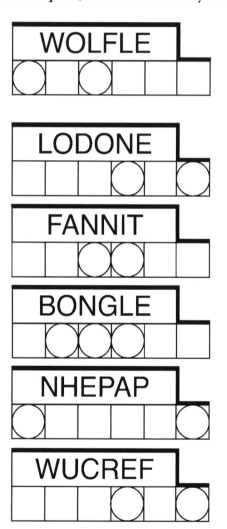

WOLFLE

LODONE

FANNIT

BONGLE

NHEPAP

WUCREF

Hey!
Watch where
you're going!

WHEN THE WITCH WAS
BUMPED IN MIDFLIGHT,
SHE – – –

Now arrange the circled letters to form the surprise answer, as suggested by the above cartoon.

Print answer here

○○○○ ○○○ THE ○○○○○○○

JUMBLE®

Unscramble these six Jumbles, one letter to each square, to form six ordinary words.

BOMERY

REGAHN

BIGTAM

CUPONE

FRAIDT

CELFIK

LOADING ZONE

This will cost me $50

SOUNDS GOOD WHEN LEAVING YOUR CAR IN AN ILLEGAL SPACE.

Now arrange the circled letters to form the surprise answer, as suggested by the above cartoon.

Print answer here

JUMBLE®

Unscramble these six Jumbles, one letter
to each square, to form six ordinary words.

GUNTOE

CUNESS

LOORIE

GRUIFE

RAMPUK

BLOUFE

CLERK OF THE COURT

Counselor

Hello,
counselor

WHAT THE OPPOSING
LAWYERS HAD
WHEN THEY
FILED THEIR CASE.

Now arrange the circled letters to form
the surprise answer, as suggested by the
above cartoon.

Print answer here

A " ⬤⬤⬤⬤⬤ " ⬤⬤⬤⬤⬤⬤⬤⬤⬤

JUMBLE®

Unscramble these six Jumbles, one letter to each square, to form six ordinary words.

GLENET

LEZZUP

KONYED

DIBRYH

HYNTAS

LIFFUT

Al keeps them loose

I'm next

WHY THE TEAM HIRED THE MASSAGE THERAPIST.

Now arrange the circled letters to form the surprise answer, as suggested by the above cartoon.

Print answer here

☐☐ ☐☐☐☐☐ A " ☐☐☐☐☐ "

JUMBLE®

Unscramble these six Jumbles, one letter
to each square, to form six ordinary words.

NIVIET

RASITE

HOWTRY

STYLUB

GLIEGG

NELPOY

That's it

He didn't
miss a trick

Something for
everyone

WHEN THE SMALL PRINT
IN THE LAWYER'S
WILL WAS READ, IT
ENDED UP ---

Now arrange the circled letters to form
the surprise answer, as suggested by the
above cartoon.

Print answer here

JUMBLE®

Unscramble these six Jumbles, one letter
to each square, to form six ordinary words.

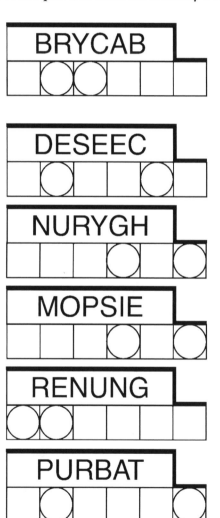

BRYCAB

DESEEC

NURYGH

MOPSIE

RENUNG

PURBAT

Every view
is different

I can't get
enough
of it

WHAT THE TOURISTS
DID WHEN THEY
VISITED THE
GRAND CANYON .

Now arrange the circled letters to form
the surprise answer, as suggested by the
above cartoon.

Print answer here

" ⬡⬡⬡⬡⬡⬡ " ON
ITS   ⬡⬡⬡⬡⬡⬡⬡

JUMBLE

Unscramble these six Jumbles, one letter
to each square, to form six ordinary words.

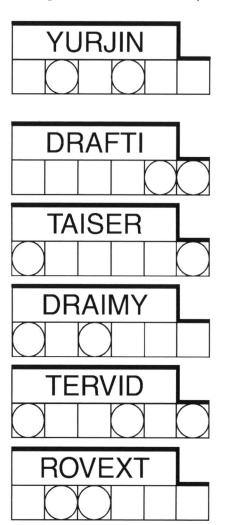

YURJIN

DRAFTI

TAISER

DRAIMY

TERVID

ROVEXT

That's our
new professor

He's an expert
on the past

6/28

THE HISTORIAN
RETURNED
TO HIS ALMA MATER
BECAUSE HE WAS A---

Now arrange the circled letters to form
the surprise answer, as suggested by the
above cartoon.

Print answer here

"◯◯◯◯◯◯◯" ◯◯◯◯◯◯◯◯

JUMBLE®

Unscramble these six Jumbles, one letter
to each square, to form six ordinary words.

BLOWEB

YIHRTT

GRYPIN

TENNIT

DRYBAN

YALERN

Marla hates
to lose

GYMNASTIC FINALS

WHEN THE GYMNAST
COMPETED IN THE
FLOOR EXERCISE,
SHE WAS ---

Now arrange the circled letters to form
the surprise answer, as suggested by the
above cartoon.

Print answer here

" ☐☐☐☐ " ON ☐☐☐☐☐☐☐☐

183

Answers

1. **Jumbles:** WEAVE UPPER MARKET FORMAL
   Answer: They loved their adopted pet — "FURREVER"

2. **Jumbles:** EXERT DWARF BISECT SALMON
   Answer: Having chocolate on her mind gave her — SWEET DREAMS

3. **Jumbles:** BLESS SCOUR BESIDE CREAMY
   Answer: The dogs that didn't get along were — CROSS-BREEDS

4. **Jumbles:** LIGHT AGILE LOCKET MANNER
   Answer: When the kids kept asking questions, their mom was — ALL "NO-ING"

5. **Jumbles:** GIVEN DIVOT SAFETY ABRUPT
   Answer: After wearing his uniform for three days straight, Beetle was — FATIGUED

6. **Jumbles:** FLUID PINCH EXOTIC BEMOAN
   Answer: The repairman was single and his customers wanted to — FIX HIM UP

7. **Jumbles:** AFTER DRAFT APLOMB STOOGE
   Answer: He wanted to fish from the pier, but the marine mammals had it — SEALED OFF

8. **Jumbles:** DOUBT CRAWL CANCEL UPROOT
   Answer: He thought he knew how many vampires were there, but he forgot to — COUNT DRACULA

9. **Jumbles:** FORAY SNUCK BLIGHT OUTING
   Answer: He was told his billboard would be up in time for his grand opening, but there was — NO SIGN OF IT

10. **Jumbles:** ALIVE NACHO EXTENT ORIGIN
    Answer: When St. Peter took a day off from his job at the Pearly Gates, he was — IN HEAVEN

11. **Jumbles:** BEVEL ISSUE DREAMY AFRAID
    Answer: The eagle planned to escape from his cage at the zoo because he wanted to be — FREE AS A BIRD

12. **Jumbles:** ONION MOMMY INDIGO EXCEED
    Answer: When they found gold in the cavern, the owner of the land said — MINE MINE MINE

13. **Jumbles:** STALL HENCE IRONIC FUNNEL
    Answer: Before DVD's, the idea of putting a whole movie on a disc seemed — UN-"REEL"-ISTIC

14. **Jumbles:** STASH MIGHT PREFIX NOTIFY
    Answer: The backup quarterback was — PASSING TIME

15. **Jumbles:** ADMIT PLUME ORNERY HUMANE
    Answer: The tree wasn't growing coconuts like it should, and in order to find out why, they hired a — PALM READER

16. **Jumbles:** TRULY REBEL POLISH LOUNGE
    Answer: When her plum tree dried up due to summer heat, she decided to — PRUNE IT

17. **Jumbles:** MOTTO RAINY WRITER INVOKE
    Answer: She let her husband make something with her yarn, but he was a — "KNITWIT"

18. **Jumbles:** DIZZY NOTCH HIGHER GARBLE
    Answer: The keyboard player at the church was — ORGAN-IZED

19. **Jumbles:** TOPAZ PHOTO FLAUNT PARDON
    Answer: The new shoe company was gaining a — FOOTHOLD

20. **Jumbles:** DROOP MULCH GALLEY FORBID
    Answer: He didn't make a good shoe salesman because he was a — LOAFER

21. **Jumbles:** SHOWN TREND RATHER ONWARD
    Answer: The knight bought his armor at the — "HARD-WEAR" STORE

22. **Jumbles:** FORCE DRANK WALNUT CHROME
    Answer: He made scrambled eggs at the — CRACK OF DAWN

23. **Jumbles:** ITCHY RISKY CAMPUS INDUCE
    Answer: Kathy Bates and James Caan were happy as could be to be — IN MISERY

24. **Jumbles:** TRUMP UNDUE PERSON ACTUAL
    Answer: The fact that she was a good mom was — APPARENT

25. **Jumbles:** ELDER BLESS AFLOAT UPROOT
    Answer: The couch had turned into a — SLEEPER SOFA

26. **Jumbles:** BATCH GLAZE DOODLE CACTUS
    Answer: The service at the comedy club was so bad that it was — LAUGHABLE

27. **Jumbles:** ELECT ANKLE COFFEE OUTWIT
    Answer: The tire repairman charged a — FLAT FEE

28. **Jumbles:** BLIMP SHOVE INFUSE IODINE
    Answer: When his twin brother started mimicking him, he was — BESIDE HIMSELF

29. **Jumbles:** DITCH RIVER ALPACA EATERY
    Answer: He knew he'd fallen in love at first sight at the marathon when his — HEART RACED

30. **Jumbles:** ABATE FOCAL COUPLE FERVOR
    Answer: When the instructor didn't charge for the parachute lesson, it was a — FREE FALL

31. **Jumbles:** BOUND IRONY PROFIT FEMALE
    Answer: When he spotted the perfect evergreen tree at the nursery, he — PINED FOR IT

32. **Jumbles:** GRANT COVET INVITE UNFAIR
    Answer: The butcher shop's new employee wasn't — CUTTING IT

33. **Jumbles:** VISOR TRULY HYMNAL ENOUGH
    Answer: The couple's Valentine's Day was — LOVELY

34. **Jumbles:** DIVOT LOGIC FIRMLY ENGAGE
    Answer: The start-up clock company would be successful — ALL IN GOOD TIME

35. **Jumbles:** FIGHT AVOID LOCKET GOBBLE
    Answer: Kicking the ball between the uprights to win the game was his — FIELD GOAL

36. **Jumbles:** EAGLE UNITY OBLONG ARMORY
    Answer: The pennant company was having a — BANNER YEAR

37. **Jumbles:** ADMIT ARENA ITALIC NEPHEW
    Answer: When she wasn't working her 9-to-5 job, she studied acting — PART-TIME

38. **Jumbles:** AWOKE IRONY MOTION THEORY
    Answer: When Tabitha Spruce met Stephen King in college, she met — MR. "WRITE"

39. **Jumbles:** TAKEN TOPAZ INNING SUMMER
    Answer: The farmer's cornfield labyrinth was — A-MAIZE-ING

40. **Jumbles:** ALBUM DIGIT BOTANY INVITE
    Answer: When it came to protecting their castle, they were — "MOAT-IVATED"

41. **Jumbles:** ABATE UPPER INJURE SCREWY
    Answer: Their drive along the Mediterranean gave them a chance to enjoy the — "SEA-NERY"

42. **Jumbles:** GRIME BLURB ADJOIN INVENT
    Answer: Boo-boo liked being Yogi's sidekick, except when Yogi was being — OVERBEARING

43. **Jumbles:** CURRY PANTS EQUATE PARLOR
Answer: The novice mountain climber needed to —
LEARN THE ROPES

44. **Jumbles:** SALAD HEDGE EXCEED SAFETY
Answer: His hope of winning the sprint was about to be —
DASHED

45. **Jumbles:** CHESS GUILT PROVEN TOPPLE
Answer: Her fear of going to bed in the dark made their
daughter a — LIGHT SLEEPER

46. **Jumbles:** OOMPH MAMBO TRUDGE BYLINE
Answer: He used this to recall facts about his first computer
— HIS GOOD MEMORY

47. **Jumbles:** YOKEL DRIFT IGUANA WETTER
Answer: You can win at golf without cheating, if you win the
— FAIR WAY

48. **Jumbles:** UTTER SKUNK RUNNER SAFARI
Answer: The park started charging for rock climbing because
it wasn't — RISK-FREE

49. **Jumbles:** INEPT IMAGE RODENT SALMON
Answer: The experienced waitress gave the new hire —
GOOD TIPS

50. **Jumbles:** ROUND AUDIO HERBAL HICCUP
Answer: When she went into labor on the plane, she knew
her baby would be — AIR-BORN

51. **Jumbles:** PUPPY ALIAS UNWISE GIGGLE
Answer: The electrician would get done if he kept —
PLUGGING AWAY

52. **Jumbles:** WOOZY ICING RADIUS ICONIC
Answer: The astrologer's new billboard was —
A ZODIAC SIGN

53. **Jumbles:** SILKY INPUT RELENT HYMNAL
Answer: If the pickpocket was going to steal the man's
pocket watch, he would need to — TAKE HIS TIME

54. **Jumbles:** IMAGE VERGE DRAGON AURORA
Answer: The storm heading toward the cemetery created —
GRAVE DANGER

55. **Jumbles:** AWAIT RATIO PALACE THRASH
Answer: Even though he no longer had a use for his comb,
he wasn't going to — PART WITH IT

56. **Jumbles:** HOBBY BLURB MUFFLE TRENDY
Answer: With each glass of champagne, the party guest was
becoming — MORE BUBBLY

57. **Jumbles:** FRONT NIECE SHOULD MAGPIE
Answer: When he answered his phone while mountain
climbing, he said — HANG ON

58. **Jumbles:** USHER GROVE UTOPIA PIGLET
Answer: The waterfowl in Lisbon were this —
"PORTU-GEESE"

59. **Jumbles:** SKIMP BLEND NEURON LUNACY
Answer: When the pig made cookies, she was this — BAKIN'

60. **Jumbles:** UNCLE GRAPH AFRAID POCKET
Answer: The special on the wrapping paper, bows, tape and
scissors was this — A PACKAGE DEAL

61. **Jumbles:** ANKLE CARGO PEWTER ANGINA
Answer: How the fishing fleet caught its daily limit —
BY "NET"-WORKING

62. **Jumbles:** MESSY VIPER SKEWER FOSSIL
Answer: Means nothing in tennis but could mean a lot in
romance — LOVE AND KISSES

63. **Jumbles:** YOKEL GAILY EIGHTY TRUANT
Answer: How the craft class described their group —
TIGHTLY KNIT

64. **Jumbles:** LYING CHAMP POETRY ABOUND
Answer: What the newlyweds considered the wedding bells
— AP-PEALING

65. **Jumbles:** THINK GNARL DIGEST ROTATE
Answer: What an undercooked steak is in a swank restaurant
— A "RARE" SIGHT

66. **Jumbles:** DOWDY POPPY FILLET AMOEBA
Answer: What she did when she couldn't manage her hair —
BLEW HER TOP

67. **Jumbles:** RAPID DADDY BUREAU PERSON
Answer: What happens when you spend money like water
— IT DRIES UP

68. **Jumbles:** CRAZY ALBUM DABBLE WOBBLE
Answer: How mama's scolding left the young whale —
BLUBBERY

69. **Jumbles:** CHAFE ODDLY PASTRY SPORTY
Answer: What the transportation expert was known as —
A ROADS SCHOLAR

70. **Jumbles:** SOAPY GRIEF NICELY DUPLEX
Answer: The computer operator attributed his bad back to
this — A FLOPPY DISC

71. **Jumbles:** BUSHY INEPT FROLIC INNING
Answer: What a row of boxers might be called —
A PUNCH LINE

72. **Jumbles:** MUSIC GASSY JUNGLE SMOKER
Answer: What the musicians often called their breakfast —
A JAM SESSION

73. **Jumbles:** MINER PIETY BUSHEL PICKET
Answer: How the determined dieter overcame his weight
gain — HE KEPT HIS CHINS UP

74. **Jumbles:** CHAOS FEINT BUTLER INJECT
Answer: Why he got involved in the bird business —
TO FEATHER HIS NEST

75. **Jumbles:** IDIOT BASIN CORPSE NIBBLE
Answer: How the visitors reacted to the sponge diver's
lecture — THEY WERE ABSORBED

76. **Jumbles:** HUSKY DOILY ABDUCT HELPER
Answer: What it takes to be a successful butcher —
LOTS OF PLUCK

77. **Jumbles:** DANDY AUDIT ENDURE WALLOP
Answer: What the watch repairman did in his leisure
moments — HE UNWOUND

78. **Jumbles:** LANKY BARGE INLAND HEREBY
Answer: Often the excuse for a fender bender —
A BAD BRAKE

79. **Jumbles:** NOISY FAUNA ORIGIN ANSWER
Answer: What the chef said his apprentice needed plenty
of — "SEASON"-ING

80. **Jumbles:** STEED GUESS PRYING LARYNX
Answer: What mom used on the knitted sweater —
A STRING OF "PURLS"

81. **Jumbles:** BLAZE DAISY CALIPH ZINIA
Answer: Something that cooks do when orders get backed
up — THEY SIZZLE

82. **Jumbles:** LILAC CHANT ENTICE SINGLE
Answer: What you sometimes get from the radio — STATIC

83. **Jumbles:** SYLPH ENACT TORRID DRAGON
Answer: Why the medical student had trouble studying the
stomach — IT WAS HARD TO DIGEST

84. **Jumbles:** PIECE WHOSE GENDER STURDY
Answer: How the cleaner felt when business got slow —
DE-PRESSED

85. **Jumbles:** TARRY VALVE GRATIS SULTRY
Answer: What the church remodeler does —
HE ALTERS ALTARS

86. **Jumbles:** HOVEL WHOOP JESTER NOTIFY
Answer: What they thought their boat was — "SEE" WORTHY

87. **Jumbles:** JOUST AFIRE ENCORE POTENT
Answer: How the podiatrist kept track of his patients — WITH FOOTNOTES

88. **Jumbles:** GROIN LOOSE INVERT RARELY
Answer: What the gamblers were doing on the casino boat — ROLLIN' ON THE RIVER

89. **Jumbles:** APRON MOUSE PODIUM CLENCH
Answer: What helped keep her dry in the rain — HER "PUMPS"

90. **Jumbles:** ALIVE DAILY AIRWAY MAROON
Answer: The route they took to grandma's house — THE "WAIL"ROAD

91. **Jumbles:** GLORY HEDGE MATRON LIQUID
Answer: Playing with her puppy left her like this — DOG "TIRED"

92. **Jumbles:** PYLON SWOON EROTIC LAVISH
Answer: Another name for an eye doctor — A "VISION"-ARY

93. **Jumbles:** GLAND PRIOR NOUGAT AUBURN
Answer: What he considered his job — A GRIND

94. **Jumbles:** SHYLY VISOR VESTRY GHETTO
Answer: What the romantic snake offered the cute serpent — LOVE AND HISSES

95. **Jumbles:** MOUSY FAINT EXTANT JAUNTY
Answer: The only thing the detective was interested in — JUST THE "FAX"

96. **Jumbles:** BATCH PERKY BANISH WEDGED
Answer: What you might call the gambling ship's card dealers — DECK HANDS

97. **Jumbles:** AWFUL GRIME DAMASK SUPERB
Answer: What the military managed to achieve — AN ARMS BUILDUP

98. **Jumbles:** COMET FORAY INVEST TUXEDO
Answer: How visitors described the forest — "TREE"-MENDOUS

99. **Jumbles:** AWASH VILLA SOCKET JOYOUS
Answer: The jailer made sure these were always in place — HIS LOCKS

100. **Jumbles:** TWEET DITTY TINKLE PARITY
Answer: What the crochet club called their comedian — THE KNIT WIT

101. **Jumbles:** SMACK OPERA ASSAIL HOMAGE
Answer: How you might smell the beginning of a romance — WITH AN "A-ROMA"

102. **Jumbles:** COLIC KINKY UNSAID PLAQUE
Answer: "Jump, miss" — SKIP

103. **Jumbles:** BIRCH GLAND OUTCRY RAGLAN
Answer: This is the least you can do! — NOTHING

104. **Jumbles:** TABOO CHEEK BLUISH INDOOR
Answer: If it's still there, there isn't any — ACTION

105. **Jumbles:** DAUNT CHAMP SUBMIT INVERT
Answer: Background material for an artist — CANVAS

106. **Jumbles:** BANJO TYPED HANDLE FASTEN
Answer: They sometimes work around the clock on the farm — "HANDS"

107. **Jumbles:** MERCY FAITH NICELY GOITER
Answer: Tell this guy to go to blazes — and you'll get a response out of him! — A FIREMAN

108. **Jumbles:** NOVEL GRIPE ABSORB DAINTY
Answer: Provides the main course on board ship — THE NAVIGATOR

109. **Jumbles:** DINER LOVER ABOUND BRANDY
Answer: A puzzling way to make holes — RIDDLE

110. **Jumbles:** ABATE RANCH BIKINI TURNIP
Answer: You wouldn't want to go to the doctor if you suffered from this — INERTIA

111. **Jumbles:** LOOSE ALIAS MATRON GOSPEL
Answer: Festivity with a gal! — A GALA

112. **Jumbles:** OWING CHOKE SLOGAN IRONIC
Answer: It's definitely a racket! — NOISE

113. **Jumbles:** VISOR ETUDE AGENCY NATURE
Answer: What they drove back in — REVERSE

114. **Jumbles:** LATCH BELIE SHAKEN MEMOIR
Answer: Might BE in the sale at the fur shop — "SA-B-LE"

115. **Jumbles:** YOUNG FANCY HAPPEN LEVITY
Answer: Makes many a slip! — NYLON

116. **Jumbles:** IGLOO VALOR MALLET ACHING
Answer: Why leaving your old home might be emotionally disturbing — IT'S "MOVING"

117. **Jumbles:** ONION PLAIT HOTBED TOUCHY
Answer: What you think is yours — OPINION

118. **Jumbles:** DANDY TWEET BOTHER RITUAL
Answer: How to offer them better meat — "TENDER" IT

119. **Jumbles:** ACRID DRAFT IMPAIR ENZYME
Answer: What a doctor puts on before he starts working — AN "M D"

120. **Jumbles:** MAUVE ITCHY FUTURE GRIMLY
Answer: They do like each other — IMITATE

121. **Jumbles:** NEWLY BARON POLLEN AUTUMN
Answer: Make nothing of it! — ANNUL

122. **Jumbles:** DROOP EXULT BEWARE VOLUME
Answer: This is owing to being late — OVERDUE

123. **Jumbles:** MUSIC TRIPE DAWNED ANEMIA
Answer: What you'd expect from a little devil — "IMP-UDENCE"

124. **Jumbles:** SUAVE HANDY POWDER LIQUID
Answer: What a top hat might make — YOUR HEAD SPIN

125. **Jumbles:** VERVE TOOTH DEVICE BANNER
Answer: Try and give this to a prisoner — THE VERDICT

126. **Jumbles:** EPOCH APART BETAKE FLORAL
Answer: Might mean some drip let the secrets out — A "LEAK"

127. **Jumbles:** BATHE PAYEE CLOUDY ICEBOX
Answer: Ran down the beach — EBBED

128. **Jumbles:** INLET HAVEN THORAX GAMBOL
Answer: As long as you are — it's yours — HEIGHT

129. **Jumbles:** LUSTY FENCE POROUS GRISLY
Answer: From a ruse, you can make certain of this — SURE

130. **Jumbles:** OPIUM ENJOY REALTY LIZARD
Answer: Once aroused you may lose it! — YOUR TEMPER

131. **Jumbles:** PROBE TARDY BALLAD GIBBON
Answer: What he was was apparent — A PARENT

132. **Jumbles:** BEGUN SAVOR GARISH PROFIT
Answer: Today's answer will dawn on you tomorrow — SUNRISE

133. **Jumbles:** ERUPT GAUGE PASTRY INCOME
Answer: They might be carried by cards — GREETINGS

134. **Jumbles:** BUXOM INKED CAUCUS FALTER
Answer: This might be composed of mud and air — RADIUM

135. **Jumbles:** AWOKE MINOR CLIENT BONNET
Answer: You just can't shut your eyes to this! — LOOK

136. **Jumbles:** DAISY CREEL AROUSE STURDY
Answer: They insure the correct delivery of speeches — ADDRESSES

137. **Jumbles:** VIGIL WAKEN THRESH LAWYER
Answer: This view may help you get a job — AN INTERVIEW

138. **Jumbles:** IRATE VALUE SKEWER BLEACH
Answer: Might be straining to do a job — A SIEVE

139. **Jumbles:** DIRTY AGING PLACID VIOLIN
Answer: This is used in summing up — ADDITION

140. **Jumbles:** PUPIL HOVEL DISCUS QUARTZ
Answer: This would describe a high-spirited chiseler —
"CHIPPER"

141. **Jumbles:** DOUSE GROIN LAYOFF PRAYER
Answer: What might be hidden in a garden? — DANGER

142. **Jumbles:** FAMED ENVOY OCCULT PULPIT
Answer: Sometimes carries poison and sounds awful —
"VIAL"

143. **Jumbles:** ELITE SNARL OPIATE MORTAR
Answer: Theater performances not open to the public —
OPERATIONS

144. **Jumbles:** LANKY AFIRE CRAVAT FICKLE
Answer: You have to be it with the first letter before you can
be it without the first — L-EARNER

145. **Jumbles:** AORTA FAULT ALWAYS JACKAL
Answer: How not to leave a door if you don't want them to
steal a vase — "A-JAR"

146. **Jumbles:** ADAPT SLANT COUPLE ROSARY
Answer: How to get good looks — STARE

147. **Jumbles:** PIKER GUEST MISUSE HUNGRY
Answer: They contract to give you a comfortable ride —
SPRINGS

148. **Jumbles:** LYRIC FAVOR BUTANE MEDLEY
Answer: How the fat man spoke — BROADLY

149. **Jumbles:** LURID SWAMP MARVEL CALIPH
Answer: Completely tied up in postal regulations! —
PARCELS

150. **Jumbles:** IRONY SAUTE PEPSIN FARINA
Answer: Goes off to report trouble — A SIREN

151. **Jumbles:** FORCE ARBOR MARROW PLEDGE
Answer: Might be mad about the engine — "LOCO"

152. **Jumbles:** ANNUL SCOUT GRATIS MIDWAY
Answer: It's more usual to have only half of this — TWINS

153. **Jumbles:** VAGUE TRILL FAULTY BODICE
Answer: This would indicate that someone has just stopped
smoking — A LIVE BUTT

154. **Jumbles:** TAFFY OLDER PAUNCH BLAZER
Answer: This is the result of a musical strike — A TONE

155. **Jumbles:** WHILE DOGMA PICNIC BROOCH
Answer: Why she married the artist —
SHE WAS DRAWN TO HIM

156. **Jumbles:** DEPOT ANKLE MORBID PLAGUE
Answer: Late in bed and delayed — "BE-LATE-ED"

157. **Jumbles:** CHAIR PATIO FAMOUS MANAGE
Answer: Twice a mother — MAMA

158. **Jumbles:** DRAMA LINGO MODERN CELERY
Answer: You have to have grounds to be this —
A LANDLORD

159. **Jumbles:** NUDGE ANNOY URCHIN BRIDLE
Answer: What the frustrated racehorse was always getting
— THE RUNAROUND

160. **Jumbles:** WHOSE PARTY NOVICE CANINE
Answer: This might be responsible for a certain coolness at
the top — A SNOWCAP

161. **Jumbles:** UNWISE FRUGAL THROWN IODINE SCULPT AFLOAT
Answer: Building a moat around the castle was a —
LAST-DITCH EFFORT

162. **Jumbles:** THRIVE DONKEY INFAMY SAFETY THRASH DUPLEX
Answer: Sinking the 50-footer for eagle —
"PUTT" HIM IN THE LEAD

163. **Jumbles:** IMMUNE HAMMER WISDOM NIMBLE FORMAT
VACANT
Answer: After the deer had a baby, they —
FAWNED OVER HIM

164. **Jumbles:** RADISH THRIVE PALACE STENCH CLOSET UNWISE
Answer: The meteorologist called in to work sick so that she
could get — UNDER THE WEATHER

165. **Jumbles:** SHAKEN UPROAR BIGGER INFUSE RADIAL ABRUPT
Answer: When the jackhammer was invented, it was —
GROUNDBREAKING

166. **Jumbles:** VANISH HARDER ENGAGE CLERGY MORTAL
UTMOST
Answer: When it came to the new pair of shoes, she was —
HEAD OVER HEELS

167. **Jumbles:** SURVEY UNSURE THEORY SWATCH UNRULY
SAVORY
Answer: After such a dreary winter and wet spring, the dad
was happy to see some — "SONNY" WEATHER

168. **Jumbles:** COSTLY FAMILY PELTED RENOWN JACKAL PULSAR
Answer: When the Giants leave the Big Apple for an away
game, they — FLY NEW YORK JETS

169. **Jumbles:** LIQUID ZEALOT APIECE ANYHOW COZIER FEDORA
Answer: When they carved the Jumble into granite, they
made a — HARD PUZZLE

170. **Jumbles:** ACQUIT GRAMPA TRICKY TURNIP PICKUP WRITER
Answer: Taking photographs of your vacation makes it
easier to do this later — PICTURE IT

171. **Jumbles:** DIVERT INJURY VORTEX ABDUCT PATTER WINNOW
Answer: What the passengers experienced when the
snowstorm hit — A "WINTER-UPTION"

172. **Jumbles:** MAKEUP DEPICT SAVORY CHERUB CIPHER RANCOR
Answer: What a bank teller will do before she'll cash your
check — CHECK YOUR CASH

173. **Jumbles:** FELLOW NOODLE INFANT BELONG HAPPEN
CURFEW
Answer: When the witch was bumped in midflight, she —
FLEW OFF THE HANDLE

174. **Jumbles:** EMBRYO HANGER GAMBIT POUNCE ADRIFT FICKLE
Answer: Sounds good when leaving your car in an illegal
space — "FINE" FOR PARKING

175. **Jumbles:** TONGUE CENSUS ORIOLE FIGURE MARKUP BEFOUL
Answer: What the opposing lawyers had when they filed
their case — A "BRIEF" ENCOUNTER

176. **Jumbles:** GENTLE PUZZLE DONKEY HYBRID SHANTY FITFUL
Answer: Why the team hired the massage therapist —
HE FILLED A "KNEAD"

177. **Jumbles:** INVITE SATIRE WORTHY SUBTLY GIGGLE OPENLY
Answer: When the small print in the lawyer's will was read, it
ended up — SPLITTING "HEIRS"

178. **Jumbles:** CRABBY SECEDE HUNGRY IMPOSE GUNNER
Answer: What the tourists did when they visited the Grand
Canyon— "GORGED" ON ITS BEAUTY

179. **Jumbles:** INJURY ADRIFT SATIRE MYRIAD DIVERT VORTEX
Answer: The historian returned to his alma mater because
he was a — "FORMER" STUDENT

180. **Jumbles:** WOBBLE THIRTY PRYING INTENT BRANDY NEARLY
Answer: When the gymnast competed in the floor exercise,
she was — "BENT" ON WINNING

Need More Jumbles®?

Jumble® Books

More than 175 puzzles each!

Cowboy Jumble®
• ISBN: 978-1-62937-355-3

Jammin' Jumble®
• ISBN: 978-1-57243-844-6

Java Jumble®
• ISBN: 978-1-60078-415-6

Jet Set Jumble®
• ISBN: 978-1-60078-353-1

Jolly Jumble®
• ISBN: 978-1-60078-214-5

Jumble® Anniversary
• ISBN: 987-1-62937-734-6

Jumble® Ballet
• ISBN: 978-1-62937-616-5

Jumble® Birthday
• ISBN: 978-1-62937-652-3

Jumble® Celebration
• ISBN: 978-1-60078-134-6

Jumble® Champion
• ISBN: 978-1-62937-870-1

Jumble® Coronation
• ISBN: 978-1-62937-976-0

Jumble® Cuisine
• ISBN: 978-1-62937-735-3

Jumble® Drag Race
• ISBN: 978-1-62937-483-3

Jumble® Ever After
• ISBN: 978-1-62937-785-8

Jumble® Explorer
• ISBN: 978-1-60078-854-3

Jumble® Explosion
• ISBN: 978-1-60078-078-3

Jumble® Fever
• ISBN: 978-1-57243-593-3

Jumble® Galaxy
• ISBN: 978-1-60078-583-2

Jumble® Garden
• ISBN: 978-1-62937-653-0

Jumble® Genius
• ISBN: 978-1-57243-896-5

Jumble® Geography
• ISBN: 978-1-62937-615-8

Jumble® Getaway
• ISBN: 978-1-60078-547-4

Jumble® Gold
• ISBN: 978-1-62937-354-6

Jumble® Health
• ISBN: 978-1-63727-085-1

Jumble® Jackpot
• ISBN: 978-1-57243-897-2

Jumble® Jailbreak
• ISBN: 978-1-62937-002-6

Jumble® Jambalaya
• ISBN: 978-1-60078-294-7

Jumble® Jitterbug
• ISBN: 978-1-60078-584-9

Jumble® Journey
• ISBN: 978-1-62937-549-6

Jumble® Jubilation
• ISBN: 978-1-62937-784-1

Jumble® Jubilee
• ISBN: 978-1-57243-231-4

Jumble® Juggernaut
• ISBN: 978-1-60078-026-4

Jumble® Kingdom
• ISBN: 978-1-62937-079-8

Jumble® Knockout
• ISBN: 978-1-62937-078-1

Jumble® Madness
• ISBN: 978-1-892049-24-7

Jumble® Magic
• ISBN: 978-1-60078-795-9

Jumble® Mania
• ISBN: 978-1-57243-697-8

Jumble® Marathon
• ISBN: 978-1-60078-944-1

Jumble® Masterpiece
• ISBN: 978-1-62937-916-6

Jumble® Neighbor
• ISBN: 978-1-62937-845-9

Jumble® Parachute
• ISBN: 978-1-62937-548-9

Jumble® Party
• ISBN: 978-1-63727-008-0

Jumble® Safari
• ISBN: 978-1-60078-675-4

Jumble® Sensation
• ISBN: 978-1-60078-548-1

Jumble® Skyscraper
• ISBN: 978-1-62937-869-5

Jumble® Symphony
• ISBN: 978-1-62937-131-3

Jumble® Theater
• ISBN: 978-1-62937-484-0

Jumble® Time Machine: 1972
• ISBN: 978-1-63727-082-0

Jumble® Trouble
• ISBN: 978-1-62937-917-3

Jumble® University
• ISBN: 978-1-62937-001-9

Jumble® Unleashed
• ISBN: 978-1-62937-844-2

Jumble® Vacation
• ISBN: 978-1-60078-796-6

Jumble® Wedding
• ISBN: 978-1-62937-307-2

Jumble® Workout
• ISBN: 978-1-60078-943-4

Jump, Jive and Jumble®
• ISBN: 978-1-60078-215-2

Lunar Jumble®
• ISBN: 978-1-60078-853-6

Monster Jumble®
• ISBN: 978-1-62937-213-6

Mystic Jumble®
• ISBN: 978-1-62937-130-6

Rainy Day Jumble®
• ISBN: 978-1-60078-352-4

Royal Jumble®
• ISBN: 978-1-60078-738-6

Sports Jumble®
• ISBN: 978-1-57243-113-3

Summer Fun Jumble®
• ISBN: 978-1-57243-114-0

Touchdown Jumble®
• ISBN: 978-1-62937-212-9

Oversize Jumble® Books

More than 500 puzzles!

Colossal Jumble®
• ISBN: 978-1-57243-490-5

Jumbo Jumble®
• ISBN: 978-1-57243-314-4

Jumble® Crosswords™

More than 175 puzzles!

Jumble® Crosswords™
• ISBN: 978-1-57243-347-2